# YOU Can Be in Love With

anybody and still be in love with Edie. You didn't have to stop being in love with anybody to be in love with Edie. The circle of magic that she presented was big enough to take you in.

**—DANNY FIELDS**

# GIRL ON FIRE

## BY Melissa Painter & David Weisman

CHRONICLE BOOKS
SAN FRANCISCO

# contents

Chapter Two:
NEW YORK 36

Chapter Three:
CALIFORNIA 158

Edie Sedgwick couldn't be contained. Sometimes that meant she was elusive, other times it meant she got the joke better than anyone else in the room. ★

She was an adventurer, an explorer of the future. Fueled by ghosts and demons from her past, she was the extraterrestrial girl on fire who streaked across the '60s cosmos to dazzle and enrapture, push the limits, and test the boundaries of everyone she crossed paths with in life. Yet she always remained just a tad beyond anyone's grasp. ★

We were two manic years into our movie adventure before I really felt I knew Edie. We bonded at a madhouse somewhere in some grim visiting room that smelled of bleach; it was right after the first moon-landing and at a point in the popular culture when a person's heroic qualities were measured by their fantastic escapades and the stories being told about them. Edie, charismatic demiurge and confabulator in the great oral tradition of epic adventurers, wrote her own myths—but always

A stiff price had to be paid for such immersion into another's psyche. During the process there was loss of any connection to financial stability, to any former glamour or status—the "ground control to Major Tom" moment when you're way out there in an orbit of your own, with no turning back. So far out, in fact, that only afterward did questions begin to arise about the project's moral grounding. There is a blackout in my memory about the years following Edie's death, and I didn't work in film again for nearly a decade. John Palmer, among the most naturally gifted cinematic eyes of his time, never made another movie. ★

In 1998, screenwriter Leonard Schrader invited me to a thesis class he was teaching at USC, where a student asked how I got into the movie business. I spoke about my background and collaboration with Schrader on our 1985 film *Kiss of the Spider Woman*. When it came time for questions, all hands instantly shot up. Here were a dozen graduate students of film who couldn't have cared less about my adventures with Fellini or Preminger, Vadim or Babenco, all anxious to know one thing: "What was Edie like?" ★

I was blindsided—astonished at first that they even knew who she was—then intrigued and eventually haunted by how passionately they wanted to know more. I came to understand that for years now, countless young people coming of age have discovered Edie Sedgwick and felt a strangely compelling, deeply emotional connection to her odyssey. ★

Edie ad-libs a line of dialogue in *Ciao! Manhattan* that could as well have been her own sly way of prophesying this latest predicament of hers: *"The first 15 minutes takes . . . a long time. But the second 15 minutes takes . . . forever!"* ★

Of course she was simply expressing how wiped-out she got from sitting in the sauna, waiting for a "poke," at Doctor Feelgood's office where the sequence was filmed in the spring of '67, and Warhol's "famous for 15 minutes" quote didn't surface until 1973. But this vital and seemingly perpetual need for knowing more about the real Edie, for examining why her story has now taken on such resonance for a new generation, inspired me onto a quest that led to the creation of this book. A personal epiphany for me, while immersed in interviews and photos for the project, was the realization that I myself—like most everyone else in her life—only ever really got to know a small portion of the eternal mystery that is Edie Sedgwick. ★

Edie was magnetic. She was daring, she was a rule-breaker, a trickster, ignoring the laws of society and using her own out-rageous behavior and parody to comment on the world around her. In this she was like other '60s revolutionaries such as the Diggers or the Merry Pranksters, living examples of the absurdities of the time and of the utopian ideal. ★

What was unique about Edie was that she invented a kind of fame never seen before, but treated it with a wink, as if to say: I know what this is even as it happens. She came to New York at age 21 to at once be discovered and get lost, at a time when people celebrated their peers' "willingness to go to the edge." Edie symbolized their hunger for abandon like no one else. This was both the magic of her situation and her undoing. She became an overnight phenomenon solely for being Edie. She had no songs to perform, no paintings to show, her films were obscure, and so there was only her presence and her image: the way she could stop a room by walking into it. ★

It is ironic that the first person touted for being famous for doing nothing at all thought very specifically about the purpose of her fame. Edie believed that she was living to prove that if she could survive, that if she could live openly and honestly as she battled to break out of the mold, then she could help others understand the possibilities—share who you are and let people know that you're human. She felt there were things to be done, as though she had come from a long way away, that there was a mission afoot to upset the applecart and bring a greater consciousness. She felt special. She was trying to invent a new way to live. She even believed, in a truly modern sense, that people needed to learn how to commune more with space, and with nature, and not always just on a human plane, if they were to keep up with the speed of their lives. ★

Oddly, her prophesies about her purpose and about her fame, messianic though they might sound, have been strangely fulfilled in the people for whom her story resonates and for whom the phenomenon of her fame registers as deeply authentic. She is both the harbinger of celeb-rity culture and someone who stands entirely outside of it, an artist who painted life, bravely and spontaneously, with her own hand. This book attempts to capture the sensation of standing next to Edie Sedgwick, of getting caught off guard by her, of holding her attention. All the things that people who knew her well still talk about. ★

Interviews with thirty-five of these people, many speaking publicly for the first time, appear in this book. They accompany Edie's own words—gleaned from interviews, audiotapes, films, and letters—and trace her path from her birthplace in California to Cambridge, Massachusetts, where she began her adult life, to New York City, and back to her final days in California. Biographical notes and a timeline detail the key char-acters in, and chronology of, Edie's life. Many previously unpublished images, including newly discovered ones, taken by twenty-five photog-raphers also help tell her story. The companion CD to this book was culled from tapes she made when she was 27 years old, during the writing of the second part of *Ciao! Manhattan*. They have never before been heard. ★

INTRODUCTION

# Chapter One:
# CAMBRIDGE LIFE

Edie Sedgwick arrived in Cambridge, Massachusetts, in 1963. At age 20, the world was new to her. She was living alone for the first time, in an East Coast city for the first time, and for the first time able to look at what life might offer. She was drawn to what felt authentic and vibrant. She resisted falling into any plan either her parents or proper society might have had for her, though she had yet to cultivate a philosophy to explain her instinctive choice. The Cambridge to which her family introduced her centered on Harvard University, which five generations of Sedgwick men had attended. At various times her brother Bobby, a Porcellian Club member (like all the Sedgwick men) and a Harvard graduate, was there to shepherd her. At others, she might have met her brother Jonathan's Harvard friends, some of whom were clubbies. Left to her own devices, Edie was fond of the sensation of escape. She always had been. ★

Edith Minturn Sedgwick was born on April 20, 1943, in Santa Barbara, California, to parents who had true blue blood in their background. Her mother's Boston Brahmin family drew its wealth from Union Pacific railroad money; her father's family was responsible for the prep school Groton and the *Atlantic Monthly*. Her father, a sculptor, had fled his East Coast family role as a bit of a black sheep and committed himself to the image of the rancher's life in the West with enough zeal to suggest he held no stock in proper society. On the contrary, Francis Sedgwick remained at the core an elitist who expected his eight children to succeed in the academic and business institutions he left behind. ★

Edie and her siblings had the run of two successive family ranches: Corral de Quati and Rancho La Laguna de San Francisco. At 14 months old she was put on top of a horse. As a high-spirited young tomboy she fell in love with the immense open space and its secret places, with the changes in the weather, the sensation of escape on the back of a galloping horse. As Edie's sister, Suki, would attest, Edie had a streak of *Wuthering Heights* in her. She loved violent weather, was not afraid to be alone on a mountaintop, and likewise was not afraid of her own emotional outbursts. In this way she exhibited a fierce bravery. It is an antique thing to dwell in a place where the land as far as the eye can see in every direction belongs to your father. Edie grew up in a universe of her parents' creation, isolated and rarely touched by the outside world. That universe was troubled in many ways. ★

As a young man, Edie's father had been deemed unfit to have children because of his mental instability. He had been diagnosed as manic depressive and institutionalized after a breakdown. His children came to affectionately call him "Fuzzy." ★

One family legend, according to Edie, went like this: She discovers her father making love to one of the models who posed for his sculpture. She tells her mother, Alice. Her father calls her crazy for lying and summons a doctor to sedate her and lend credence to his own charade. Whatever other injustices, real or imagined, transpired in the relationship between father and daughter, this betrayal, of being falsely pronounced crazy, left a profound mark on Edie's psyche. She would walk a line between what she could see or was willing to see and what others could see, between reality and fantasy, between what society would define as sane behavior and crazy, and between love and hate of her parents, for the rest of her life. When her father placed her at age 18 in a Connecticut mental hospital, Silver Hill, he probably saved her life, because by then Edie had begun to starve herself to death. He also

When Edie emerged from the confines of Bloomingdale, the hospital that followed Silver Hill, she found a home in Cambridge. She began studying sculpture with a private teacher, Lily Saarinen, and feeding her self-image as someone meant for, if not a career in the arts, the creative realm. She would eventually take her only sculpture, the "famous" sculpture of a horse, with her, unfinished, to New York. But while in Cambridge she managed to find the Bohemian epicenter, including a wee-hours salon at the home of a man named Ed Hood. Edie was drawn to what amused her, what she found funny and daring. She liked outrageous people best. She wanted to be challenged, to submerge herself in energy. She was juggling multiple lives, as though testing the waters of each. One night she might have a proper date and dinner, but more often than not she snuck into the Casablanca bar in pursuit of music or conversation or mischievousness. Edie was always a night person; the sleep aids she had been given in the hospital may have contributed to a pattern of insomnia that kept her chasing the ever-possible. When her friends arranged a 21st birthday fete at the Harvard Boat House, Edie danced through the evening but still found time to change her dress three times. ★

Under a sometimes flitting and light veneer, she was deeply metaphysical and introspective. She cultivated friends on whom she could rely for different things. Bartle Bull, for example, could lunch properly with her father at the Somerset Club in Boston and present himself as good husband material, even if he had no intention of tying the knot. Chase Mellen had social clout as well. Chuck Wein, or "Chuckles" as Edie christened him, indulged her desires to discuss what was real and not real about all planes of existence. Donald Lyons, a classicist whose lively intellect thrilled her, passed her books to read and, like Wein, figured largely into her New York life, becoming one of her dearest friends and dancing partners. Ed Hennessey, the cut-up who kept Edie cheerful, was the first in a series of wits who made her list of most favorite people. Dorothy Dean, Danny Fields, Gordon Baldwin, and others also would enter the world of Andy Warhol through Edie. ★

She was often among gay men, many at that time living a sort of secret life, open among each other in the world they had created, which they freely let Edie into. During the time she was in Cambridge, Edie's brother Minty hung himself while being treated at Silver Hill for a mental breakdown. It is likely that he was undergoing a "cure" for homosexuality at his parents' behest. What is certain is that the night his doctor told him he would "never get out of the hospital" he hung himself. It was the first death of a sibling that Edie was to experience, but not the last, an example of a child within her own family who had been defeated by his inability to live within the strictures of parents and society. To Edie's mind, her own version of the fight was that her father would pronounce her crazy if she did not behave. Edie did not intend to win this battle by walking neatly within the lines. ★

Edie seemed born yesterday. She seemed very bright and very eager for life, for the things of the mind and the things of the heart, and seemed like a fresh, joyous creature, experiencing life for the first time.

—DONALD LYONS

# FIRST IMPRESSIONS

She really was lovely. She needed no makeup. She had a marvelous coloring of wonderful pale skin and very dark hair and eyes.

—BARTLE BULL

There was a young man at Harvard, and what he said was, "Every boy at Harvard was trying to save Edie from herself." And that's the quality I think she had, of being quite vulnerable and quite odd, maybe sort of a little loony but very beautiful and very, very attractive. And that, more than her physical appearance, had to do with her great appeal to guys.

—FRED EBERSTADT

The first time I remember talking to her at any length was out at Ed Hood's, and there was some kind of party going on, and she and I sat on the floor at the end of a tiny little hall and talked . . . I just remember that there was this young woman who seemed to me very exotic, very fragile, and she talked a little bit about having just gotten out of the "funny farm," which was, I think, the term she used for Silver Hill . . . I noted someplace else in a journal that the word she used for crazy was cuckoo, and I think it's somewhat telling because it's sort of little-girl vocabulary and it's a way, I think, of putting aside a judgment about how serious her own mental state might have been. But she talked a little bit about Silver Hill and, for some reason or another, the conversation became rapidly quite intimate, but I think that was her naiveté at that point . . . Innocence is a better word than naiveté. About what Edie was like at that point, after she hadn't been so very many places.

—GORDON BALDWIN

I first met Edie in the middle of September in 1963 at Harvard . . . That day I had a date scheduled with a really lovely girl . . . a picnic in my favorite place, which was the cemetery on the Charles River, the Charles Cemetery . . . and the girl never showed up, she stood me up . . . and so I had this beautiful picnic in the back of my car . . . I had some wonderful French pâté. And I had fresh daiquiris . . . and a bottle of German white wine, I think it was Moselblumchen . . . So that evening I was in a nightclub called the Casablanca and I saw a friend of mine with this stunning girl, so I went over to say hello, and when he got up to get some cigarettes, I said, "Excuse me, would you like to have a picnic tomorrow?" And so we made a date for the next day, had a fantastic picnic for two or three hours. And I saw her every day after that.

—BARTLE BULL

She just seemed crazy. She was very wild and very expressive.

**—CHASE MELLEN**

The people that I knew socially in Cambridge were brilliant, they were bright . . . What we had was an ability to laugh, an ability to see the joke and the party of things, not destructively but sort of in joy, in wit. And Edie fit right in with that, she became one of us at once and became a part of us.

**—DONALD LYONS**

They were the smartest, classiest, brightest, best-looking crowd in Cambridge, that was the A-list.

**—DANNY FIELDS**

She was very much, sort of, you know, one of the interesting people in Cambridge. I asked who is this? "Oh, she's this girl, she's at the parties . . . Oh, those Sedgwicks, my God, they've had this incredible life. They've had this crazy life. And she's just come East, and she's amazing!"

**—ROBIN SEDGWICK**

**I was thinking of how when I went to Cambridge after I'd gotten out of two years of hospitals, where my parents had me committed, I went to Cambridge and I started going out a lot. And then I never came back at night at all. I was out with different men every night, practically. And my younger sister and youngest brother tried to get me committed to McClane's for my bad behavior. They thought I was really being terrible. But I didn't go** *(laugh)*.

**—EDIE**

# HOSPITAL MEMORIES

This was the police record, report, on me, given to the police by my father, written down as fact that I was homicidal, suicidal, threatening bodily harm to my sister and my mother, and that I ran around screaming naked. Well, the last part of it appealed to me, but . . . *(laugh)*

—EDIE

It was known that she had a grim background. But she was herself free, and seemed a creature of the sunlight, with a darkness behind her that we knew no details about.

—DONALD LYONS

**When I was in the hospital, I was very suicidal in a kind of blind way, I was starving to death and just 'cause I didn't want to turn out like my family showed me, you know, that's all I ever saw of people, was my own family. I wasn't allowed to associate with anyone. Oh, God. So I didn't want to live.**

**—EDIE**

I don't know that she thought she deserved to be put away in that sense. I think, like most people who are marginal, they can present themselves very well, but they also know internally that they have a little dark side.

—BARTLE BULL

**My mother denies to this day that one of my brothers' suicides was suicide, and it's on hospital and police records as suicide.**

**—EDIE**

She certainly didn't think she was any sicker than Fuzzy or the mother, and she thought Fuzzy was a control freak that had ruined the brothers and sisters, and she was the only one strong enough to fight him. She used to steal his Porsche when she was 14 and drive down the coast highway. Rebellious, right? The others wouldn't dream of it. She was the only one who did, and there was a constant idea that when she turned 21, they were really gonna have to get the doctors to try and commit her.

—CHUCK WEIN

I guess the thing was, Edie wanted to talk about the cosmos and the whole picture all the time. It was kind of a dream; it's kind of like psychedelics without the psychedelics. She was very like "talk about the planets and the stars." But, I mean, as a world, not as "look at the pretty stars." She had a kind of worldview of her own. She evidently had spent a lot of time thinking, where she'd been, institutionalized, and that was, I guess, a way of dealing with it, to be in the cosmos and think about yourself as part of that rather than the particular ratty situation on the physical plane.

—CHUCK WEIN

She had learned to separate her life a bit, both with her father and her friends.
—BARTLE BULL

MANY LIVES

She had a double life in Cambridge. She had this clubby life, you know, the guys that were in the clubs, and I . . . didn't have anything to do with that world, so I never really saw . . . She hung out with them, but I think she got very bored with them very quickly, and I saw her more at the places that I went to . . . And after the Casablanca closed everyone would go over to [Ed Hood's apartment], kind of a cross-section of people. She would show up there all the time.

—CHASE MELLEN

Edie wasn't around all the time. She would sort of disappear. Whether she disappeared into the studio or somewhere else, I don't know. I think it is possible there was a romantic involvement, but one didn't know about it.

—GORDON BALDWIN

No, no, I don't remember Bartle Bull, no. I mean, I remember Bartle Bull. I don't remember the two of them together, no.

—DONALD LYONS

We were certainly dating, yes. Oh yes.

—BARTLE BULL

Being something of a clown, I made her laugh every five minutes—or tried to. Despite her limited education, she had a keen and intelligent sense of humor. Not intellectual, but intelligent.

—ED HENNESSEY

Ed Hennessey, he was kind of a vest pocket Oscar Wilde, do you know? Very witty and so adult, by the time he was 18 he was like a 30-year-old.

—CHASE MELLEN

Occasionally she seemed very fragile and uncertain. She wasn't consistent. One evening I'd be the right kind of person for her to see, then another evening she'd go and do something else, one day she'd want to paint and work forever, a week later she wouldn't. She was obviously not yet settled in herself, she didn't know which way to jump with her day or her life.

—BARTLE BULL

Yes, I think Edie was looking for a new "family" in Cambridge, and I don't feel that we let her down. It was her Santa Barbara and New York "families" that let her down.

—ED HENNESSEY

I think that she was sort of, at the time I was seeing her, looking at three different worlds, and I was sort of one . . . that was a bit steadier perhaps, and she was meanwhile meeting people who later led her into deeper mischief.

—BARTLE BULL

It was clear she was not meant for the plan, if that was it.

—CHASE MELLEN

She was the most talented young person I've taught art to. She'd come in late and very tired. She'd have her friends come in, and pretty soon more came. She was very insecure about men, though all the men loved her. She was chic and adorable. Pretty soon my life was Edie because I couldn't do anything else.

—LILY SAARINEN

I learned what a great artist she was. I saw her sketches and her drawing, and she really had a gift for that. She would get a new teacher and they would say how brilliant she was, how wonderful she could be, and one of the distressing things about her already was that she wouldn't follow through, she wouldn't actually finish the picture, finish the sculpture. I'd say, "How is it going?" She'd say, "Well, I think I'll start again," and put it aside for a few days. She would work in fits and starts.

—BARTLE BULL

**ART**

# MOTHER AND FATHER.

When they decided to go West, they really created their own world. They created a kind of a fairy-tale world where, instead of being the fringe element, they were the center. They ran it, they were the king and queen, they could make the world anything they were. And these children grew up as courtiers in a—they grew up as playing parts in their parents' fantasy world.

—ROBIN SEDGWICK

Their kids were their subjects, they weren't their kids. They weren't their kids, I mean as we know kids. I mean . . . It's so funny, in my growing up, my mother and father were distant parents, but they were parents and you always felt safe and you always felt supported and these kids couldn't have felt safe for an instant. What was going to jump on them next from behind?

—HARRY DWIGHT SEDGWICK

I always thought Edie wanted to escape on her horse, but she couldn't get off the ranch. She was penned in. Usually it started with a battle with my father. She always felt that he would come and get her. So she could only run away on the ranch. She would just disappear into the mountains with her horse, Chub, and you never knew where she was. Then she'd come back mellowed out.

—JONATHAN SEDGWICK

Fuzzy was this wheezing, asthmatic guy who struggled through his early life and he had a, you know, he had a nervous breakdown . . . but, boy, when he got out to the ranch, he was Mr. God.

—HARRY DWIGHT SEDGWICK

One of the reasons I think she liked the sculpting lessons and all that was that she could say to the mother, "Look, I'm doing what Fuzzy does."

—CHUCK WEIN

I think she had mixed feelings about her old man, but, I mean, who wouldn't? He was a very difficult and, I think, in some social ways, even dangerous character. And he also had a great talent, and an even bigger ego than his talent . . . At a couple of Mexican churches in Southern California, where they couldn't really afford to say no, he would be generous to them, and in a couple of them he'd paint himself as Christ behind the altar.

—BARTLE BULL

The stories about her family had the nature of being secrets. I'm not quite sure why there should be secrecy, but somehow if she talked about Minty, which she didn't do much, and after Bobby's death, that somehow she was talking about something that was deep inside.

—GORDON BALDWIN

It is, of course, very significant that the sculpture, the famous sculpture, was of a horse because that's what Duke [Francis Sedgwick] sculpted . . . What kind of competition is that, that she was setting up with her father?

—GORDON BALDWIN

Yeah! It's a great big thing, a good sculpture. He made a Christ on the cross that's him, and gave it to the mission. He was actually a brilliant sculptor when he began with portrait busts. He was really good at that, but he went wild on the way to success. He was all sold on being famous and recognized in his lifetime, and as a result he just ran through his talent, and wasted it.

—EDIE

He was a complicated and complicating influence in her life. She admired, for example, his artistic energy. She admired his individuality. She admired the fact that he was his own man and nobody influenced him. But she also knew that there was a dangerous, decadent side to him. And, indeed, that attracted her to other people later in her life, the people who were witty but corrupt, artistic but corrupt.

—BARTLE BULL

# LIVING IN THE MOMENT

She just seemed to be apart from the normal concerns.

—CHASE MELLEN

She was somehow beyond the outside of the bonds, of the bounds . . . She was already in a grown-up life a little bit, and yet she was our age. She had a freedom that a lot of us didn't have yet.

—ROBIN SEDGWICK

She was a very good friend, but she was *always* late. Or a no-show. You couldn't change her, so you had to get used to it.

—ED HENNESSEY

In some ways I think Edie was ultimately, at least to me, unknowable. One didn't see where her motivation sprang from. It was hard to know about what she might want to do, but she wanted to be amused, that's for sure. She liked having lots of things happening . . . She giggled a lot.

—GORDON BALDWIN

We almost never talked seriously about our inner feelings or truths. We were interested in having fun, not philosophizing or setting goals for the future, or trying to find meaning in life.

—ED HENNESSEY

She had good manners, although she broke them more often than she used them. But, you know, she knew how to be polite.

—CHASE MELLEN

When I was at Harvard Law School, I never went to class but spent all my time with Harvard College people, playing bridge and listening to "Lili Marlene" and drinking absinthe and thinking we were so chic.

—DANNY FIELDS

She was really living day by day largely. And that also explains why she got into that wild world in New York. I don't think she was on a very clear path, but she had many talents, and a complicated background, and not a very driven sense of the future, but just a lot of abilities and enthusiasms.

—BARTLE BULL

She was tired of being pawed by men (well, *boys* is more like it). One of the main reasons Edie felt comfortable around gay boys like me was that we weren't going to bother her sexually. Besides, we were more amusing.

— ED HENNESSEY

Well, it was sexy, of course, 'cause we were all just coming out of the fifties, and most of the people that I knew or hung around with were, in one way or another, they had academic backgrounds. It was kind of a mad adventure, to be loose in this candy store. And so Edie seemed really sexy because she was sort of wild, and she was clearly available, and so that was kind of exciting. And there she was with no, you know, she wasn't studying the history of modern art and taking notes, she was just—there was always a party when she was around.

**—CHASE MELLEN**

MARRIAGE

There was always about Edie a certain spiritual quality, a certain ethereal quality. Edie was not a young girl in search of a boyfriend. Edie was not Elizabeth Bennet, though she would've been a very nice Jane Austen character. She was a flighty, darty sort. More like a Greek nymph than a winning bride.

**—DONALD LYONS**

I mean, she never set her cap for anyone or went after people . . . The thing about Edie is that not much meant anything to her. That was one of the things about her, she just had no connection to the normal. That really was part of the charm.

**—CHASE MELLEN**

A flirt, yes, a seductress, no. Her flirtatiousness, I would say, was not specific . . . When I think of someone being seductive, it's directed towards one person . . . Edie was conscious of being very attractive, but I never saw her put the moves on a specific person, so I don't think of her as a seductress, but I'm not sure that I was ever around anybody that she specifically wanted to seduce.

**—GORDON BALDWIN**

She thought, quite rightly, that her family was grooming her for a "good marriage." She was expected to meet one of her brother Jonathan's rich friends in the Porcellian—fall in love, and get married.

**—ED HENNESSEY**

They were hoping, I think, to kind of bring her to a more genteel lifestyle, and that, obviously, was doomed to failure. You could tell that right away. That wasn't gonna happen.

**—CHASE MELLEN**

Edie would say, "Oh, there's that guy . . . he really means well, but he's such a pill, but I don't want to hurt his feelings, and he's a friend of John's and keeps wanting to take me out."

**—CHUCK WEIN**

I never talked about getting married until many years later, ten years later—none of us did. I can't remember people talking about getting married like that, in those days.

**—BARTLE BULL**

We were not a future-oriented group in terms of marriage . . . We believed in falling in love, that sort of thing, but we were essentially children . . . Many fell in love with Edie.

**—DONALD LYONS**

# THE SALON—THE FIRST FACTORY

Ed Hood's was just sort of the best place to go if you wanted to have a drink at two in the morning when the bars closed. It was like Ed's was an after-hours club or something ... It was like a little salon, you know. A drunken little salon.

**—CHASE MELLEN**

Ed's bed was called Logan Field, the name of the Boston airport, because so many people landed in it. It's fair to say it was a somewhat sexually promiscuous period, and there were quite a number of people who were sleeping with both men and women. Sexual identities weren't as crystallized at that point, I think ... There's an awful amount of liquor going in all of this. I mean, he would serve drinks until no one could sit up anymore ... And this apartment is quite adjacent to the Brattle theater, and the Brattle theater is showing French New Wave films ...

**—GORDON BALDWIN**

Edie was very smart, you know, too smart. Because she came from such an insular place, she had an interesting commentary on what went by, 'cause she saw it like it was rather than in some social context like we all would.

**—CHUCK WEIN**

Everyone was very interested in conversations. They had things to say to each other, and that was a medium by which you could express yourself and learn and give and take ... It was just for its own sake, so, I don't know if that's a salon tradition, but I suspect it is. It's interesting because there's no record of that. You know, you leave no record of it so there's a kind of purity ... It's like some Zen activity.

**—CHASE MELLEN**

That's a good way to have your life. So it's about how you live your life as opposed to what mark you leave. That was everything for her. She wasn't doing anything except being alive ... She was a facilitator in a way, I suppose, too, because everyone was happy to be around her. I think she brought people together, too, in a strange way.

**—CHASE MELLEN**

She seemed snappy, kind of, she was quick, she was alert. She was quick on the uptake, do you know what I mean?

**—CHASE MELLEN**

She knew a lot of different fascinating people, and they were interesting not because they were famous or rich but because they were interesting people. They were all interesting people.

**—CHASE MELLEN**

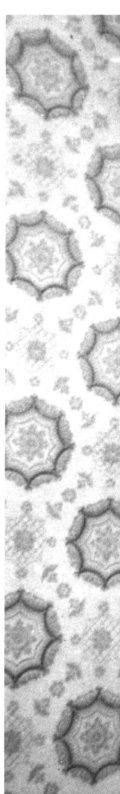

DRINK! DRINK! MORE DRINK! EVERYBODY DRINK! Geese, geese, drink!

**—EDIE**

# EDIE'S 21ST

Edie's friends threw her a grand fete for her 21st birthday party in the spring of 1964. There was music, people, dancing, and beauful dresses, three of which were worn by Edie. That night she came into a trust fund from her maternal grandmother. ★

It seemed yet another function of the laws of Edie . . . of course she should be giving an enormous party at the most glamorous place in the country!

**—DONALD LYONS**

We wanted to make such a production . . . The party was at the Harvard Boat House. Edie danced divinely. Oh, God! Everyone wanted to dance with her. She changed dresses three times during the evening. That confused a lot of people. "Do you think someone spilled a drink on her?" Then she'd be in *another* dress. "Oh, my goodness, she must have some very drunk friends. How resourceful to have extra dresses on hand if one gets spilled on!" Oh, she was something. She was something different in Cambridge!

**—ED HENNESSEY**

She's 21 . . . it's like, can she prevail to keep herself from Fuzzy shutting her away again? She was fearful. She had total fear of Fuzzy's maniacal approach. How to somehow prevail against Fuzzy locking her up again, that was entirely it.

**—CHUCK WEIN**

The word *winsome* comes to mind, that elegant, slim figure on the tabletop. It seemed so purely Fitzgeraldian. That's what made it glamorous.

**—GORDON BALDWIN**

Edie loved parties. Edie *adored* parties... It was a very comfortable party. People dancing. The moon rose out of the ocean, spiraling up in the dark. It was the final touch—a nice moon rippling on the ocean and turning everything silver. Edie was very sensitive to enchantments. She broke away from the form completely and was doing these totally free dance movements. We looked out from under the marquee, and there she was on this deserted lawn. And she was cartwheeling across it, *cartwheeling*. I remember the music dying down as the focus of attention shifted to her out there.

**—JOHN ANTHONY WALKER**

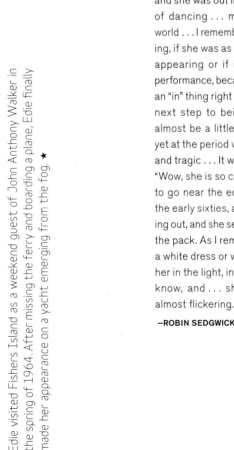

## FISHERS ISLAND

Edie visited Fishers Island as a weekend guest of John Anthony Walker in the spring of 1964. After missing the ferry and boarding a plane, Edie finally made her appearance on a yacht emerging from the fog. ★

We were all in a tent. People were drinking, partying, whatever, and suddenly I hear people saying, "Edie Sedgwick is outside the tent." So I sort of wandered over, looked out, and she was out in this field and kind of dancing... moving in her own world... I remember feeling, wondering, if she was as out of it as she was appearing or if it was part of the performance, because it certainly was an "in" thing right then. It was like the next step to being daring was to almost be a little crazy. We weren't yet at the period where it felt terrible and tragic... It was much more of a, "Wow, she is so cool, she's so daring to go near the edge."... It was still the early sixties, and we were breaking out, and she seemed to be leading the pack. As I remember, she had on a white dress or white shirt. You saw her in the light, in the moonlight, you know, and... she was turning... almost flickering.

**—ROBIN SEDGWICK**

Edie had disappeared. It was a bit spooky. Somebody said, "We saw her go swimming." She was nowhere in sight on this beach. Then somebody else said, "Is that her? Way, way out?" Edie was way out... a little dark head... such a distance. She seemed to be going under and then surfacing again. I could see the shine of her legs as she dove. It was like her dancing the night before. She was playing... totally natural and involved in the element of water; she was like a porpoise. She seemed only to exist freely in atmospheres that were removed or enchanted... most people are happy swimming by the shore, but she was happy out there."

**—JOHN ANTHONY WALKER**

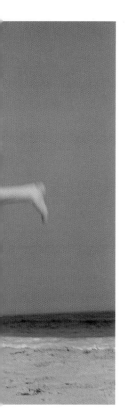

After a year I decided . . . I was going to New York to see what was really going on in the world.

**–EDIE**

She came to New York as the darling of Cambridge, and these were all rich kids. What she learned of New York, then? I don't know. She learned how to use the telephone and how to fill ashtrays with cigarette butts and steal jars of Listerine.

**–DANNY FIELDS**

# THE END OF CAMBRIDGE

# CHAPTER TWO: NEW YORK

On the eve of Edie's decision to transplant in New York, she received an $80,000 trust fund from her maternal grandmother, Julia de Forrest. It was in this grandmother's apartment on the Upper East Side, at 71st and Park, where Edie first lived when she arrived in the city. Edie took dance classes, tried out for modeling gigs, and attended society events, often with her Harvard friends in tow. Tommy Goodwin, one of her other compatriots from Cambridge, Donald Lyons, Ed Hennessey, Dorothy Dean, and Danny Fields had migrated to New York as well, as had Chuck Wein, with whom she was becoming even closer. She shopped and spent money with exuberance at her favorite restaurants, L'Aventura and the Gingerman, and frequented the clubs Ondine's and Arthur's, making a scene on their dance floors with moves all her own. When in the late fall of 1964 she moved into an apartment on East 64th, her mother arrived to furnish it in a style that included a beloved stuffed rhino from Abercrombie & Fitch that Edie dubbed "Wallow." After the discothèques closed at four, she would drive around till dawn in her grey Mercedes with Chuck Wein and others. Edie liked to drive herself; she said it was like riding a horse. ★

On a snowy night just before Christmas, Bob Dylan and Bob Neuwirth, having heard about this "terrific girl," decided they had to meet Edie, so Dylan called her. She chartered a limousine and went to meet them at The Kettle of Fish on McDougal Street. Neuwirth—a musician, painter, and close friend of Dylan's—would later play a very important role in Edie's life. Around the same time, Edie's father, who had heard about her party life and probably saw the bills, was insisting that she come to the ranch for the holidays. But her brother Bobby, a Harvard graduate student and *persona non grata* in Santa Barbara because of a feud with Fuzzy, was asking her to spend Christmas in New York with him, to have her show him the city. She decided to go west. ★

On New Year's Eve, Edie drove through a red light, causing a collision that sent her passenger, Santa Barbara friend G.J. Barker-Berfield, through the windshield and left Edie with a broken leg and lacerated forehead. The caption that ran under a wreckage photograph asked, "How did these two people step out of this car alive?" It may have been a question Edie asked herself, because Bobby, left alone on New Year's Eve in Manhattan, had run his motorcycle into the side of a bus. He died of his injuries on January 12. Edie, who quickly fled Santa Barbara for fear her father would use the accident as a way to put her back into the "loony bins," believed her brother had killed himself. She launched more intensely into spending her parents' money and behaving outlandishly. She removed her own leg cast at the discothèque Harlow to dance and used eyeliner to trace her scars. She orchestrated a series of lavish dinners, all on her dime, keeping her Cambridge friends close. ★

That March Edie met Andy Warhol. Warhol ran his own kingdom, the Factory, with a power not dissimilar to that of her father's on the ranch. Both men were artists. But the Factory allowed Edie to invent a version of herself, as a performance artist, that broke from her parents' prescribed version. In Warhol's insular community she also found a new salon, one where her magic would surface on the recordings and films that would make her a star just for being herself. ★

Edie became Andy's consort, and together they captured the imagination of the art world and the press. Their creative collaboration spanned eighteen films, countless audio tapes, and endless dramatic entrances at parties. Chuck Wein was also at Edie's side as her partner in crime, her teammate in the cinematic experiments with Warhol. Together they ventured to Paris, Madrid, Tangier, and London, where Dylan and Neuwirth were touring and filming *Dont Look Back*. ★

While she seemed to approach her notoriety playfully, as if part of a greater cosmic joke, she understood its purpose. She wanted to say something true, as she put it, in "a much more wide open space." She had spent her life feeling wildly misunderstood; this might in one fell swoop provide both the chance to right that and to free herself from her parents. The dilemma was that only spontaneity felt safe to her. Dylan, along with his legendary manager Albert Grossman (Peter, Paul and Mary; Odetta; Janis Joplin) and his management partner John Court, was drawn to Edie's star potential and wanted to help her craft a more "legitimate" career. Grossman's advice that she get away from Warhol's world clearly confused Edie, and she felt torn. At the same time the drama with her family continued, and she was constantly compelled to explain and defend her choices and ward off her father's desire to hospitalize her again. She had run through her trust fund at an alarming rate, and each promise of material gain seemed to vanish. *Jane Heir*, a larger film project that Wein and Warhol were battling over, became such a debacle that Edie began to distrust her working relationship with Chuck. Edie abruptly asked Warhol to stop showing her films in public. A movie starring Edie and Dylan was under discussion, and Grossman hired Jerry Schatzberg, renowned for his stirring images of Dylan, to photograph her. Edie and Neuwirth began a serious relationship, a first for her; she would later call him the love of her life. The Schatzberg

love for the first time, about to sign with Dylan's manager, on the verge of a genuine acting career. Edie at a peak. ★

Then she disappeared. Edie later insisted that she had holed up against the craziness of publicity. Rumors arose that she was ensconced in Woodstock with "the Dylan scene"; others claimed that she never left the city. She was appreciated in Dylan's private world for her wit and charm, her adeptness at verbal jousting. She made new friends, Dominique Robertson and Grossman's wife Sally among them. To have been one among many women versus the sole female focus of attention would have been new to her, but the drugs of choice, speed and alcohol were not. The fact is that her sojourns as a guest in Woodstock were brief and her romantic flirtation with Dylan was short but intense enough for her to have somehow inspired his poet self. But it was Bob Neuwirth, not Bob Dylan, with whom Edie was smitten. In April of 1966, she made her first non-Warhol film, with Neuwirth, which has never been seen. No one speaks more honestly than Edie about the intensity and tumult of her love for Neuwirth. It was hard for her to control these emotions once they had been unleashed. She had gone through many chaste periods and some moments of promiscuity; she feared infidelity, remoteness, abandonment. Neuwirth admonished her to stay away from drugs but she couldn't. Dylan's motorcycle crash vaporized the hope of any real-world movie project. But when Dylan's *Blonde on Blonde* album was released, it was widely believed that Edie had been the inspiration for "Just Like a Woman" and "Leopard-Skin Pill-Box Hat." Some believe that "Like a Rolling Stone" is also about her. ★

On October 17, 1966, Edie's apartment caught fire. Her rescue made front page news. She moved into the Chelsea hotel. When Edie returned to California over the Christmas holidays, her parents put her in a psychiatric ward. Neuwirth managed to save her, but by early 1967, they were drifting apart. ★

Edie turned to heroin, and then to speed to cure her heroin addiction. Her trust fund depleted, desperate to make a living as her moment was beginning to slip away, she launched bravely (or not) into *Ciao! Manhattan*, directed at first by Edie's former friend Chuck Wein, produced by David Weisman and Bob Margouleff, and paid for by Margouleff's parents. Edie and Paul America were cast as the leads. Shot in beautiful 35mm by John Palmer, *Ciao! Manhattan* was envisioned by its filmmakers as the first "above-ground/underground" movie—an American version of Claude Lelouch's *A Man and a Woman*. Two weeks into the shoot, Edie accidentally set fire to her rooms at the Chelsea hotel. ★

Footage of Edie during this period often uses distortion as a key element, yet she appears remarkably sharp, full of witty comments despite the limits to which she was pushing her body. Her exploration in the world of inner space is putting her in jeopardy. Before long she fled New York, driving non-stop to California with Sepp Donahower, a college student she met while filming *Ciao! Manhattan*, ending up at the infamous rock and roll Castle in the Hollywood Hills, then returning to New York. *Ciao* was in limbo: its unfinished script was never completely shot, leading man Paul America had disappeared (he resurfaced a year later in a rural Michigan jail on drug charges), the production had run out of money, and the film was left dangling in midair. ★

Edie participated in a Richard Leacock project with Bobby Neuwirth, who kept on trying to protect her, and a later-aborted project with L. M. Kit Carson. Soon after that she began a series of stays in psychiatric hospitals, and a string of escapes. In October 1967, while Edie was in Gracie Square Hospital, her father died of pancreatic cancer. The following April, Edie was declared dead of a near-overdose, but once again survived the impossible. In late fall of 1968, her mother brought her home to Santa Barbara. She never left California again. ★

It was 1964. The President's dead, the Beatles are coming, and something was in the air.

—DANNY FIELDS

When things became unbuttoned, when unmarried couples lived together, when people were openly gay, when people were openly taking drugs, when people were openly having sex, when people were discussing how much money they made, how much money they lost, it was very repulsive to some people, but it was very refreshing to me. I thought it was wonderful.

—FRED EBERSTADT

Things were crossing lines so fast then.

—DANNY FIELDS

The scene was tiny. We all knew each other. Cabs would not pick us up; two years later, the cab drivers *looked* like us. Three years later, the *cops* looked like us. It happened very quickly. It spread massively. But at that time it was tiny.

—RENE RICARD

I really liked being in a world where you could talk to anybody, you could be around anybody, you could talk about anything. I have to say I loved every minute of the sixties, that was what I'd been waiting for all my life.

—FRED EBERSTADT

That world was wide open at that time, the New York intellectual-slash-art-slash-social combination was . . . once you got in the room, you would just go from room to room to room to room . . .

—L. M. KIT CARSON

THE SCENE

ARTIST

I remember talking with her frequently on 63rd Street, in the mornings, for example, about where in the world we would like to go, who we would like to know, that sort of thing, mainly conversations involving utopias. She was a creature that wanted to live in utopia, as did we all. Utopia was a big house with lots of closets for Edie, lots of books for me, that sort of thing. There was something about the early sixties that impelled us to fantasy worlds.

—DONALD LYONS

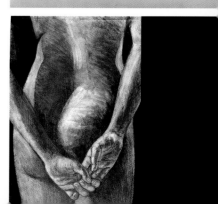

in the morning, or something like that, and it'd be, no, she couldn't sleep, she wanted to drive me back. I always wanted to walk or take a cab. She insisted. Then we'd park on 6th Avenue and talk until the sun came up, even though we'd spent all day together, and those conversations were the cosmos . . . She had a, it was an optimistic, hopeful, futuristic side . . . wouldn't it be wonderful if we could do this, this, and this.

—CHUCK WEIN

She was eager to learn, not in the way of a pupil, but somehow in the way of an artist.

—DONALD LYONS

She liked to be in unusual situations. She enjoyed them. She was amused by them.

—L. M. KIT CARSON

have—

**PAUL AMERICA:** To the city, or to the country?

**EDIE:** No, to the country, to an island. Near the sea, where I can live there happily ever after.

**PAUL AMERICA:** If that's the happy ever after, why only once in a while?

**EDIE:** Eternally . . . ?

**PAUL AMERICA:** Does it have to be? . . . I could look in a different direction.

**EDIE:** What is the direction?

**PAUL AMERICA:** Towards equality instead of control and power.

**EDIE:** That's the revolution of the youth.

**PAUL AMERICA:** Every generation tries to say that, but most of them fall in line eventually.

**EDIE:** I think something very weird's going on now, cause the power that is permitted to youth is quite extraordinary.

It's not that I'm rebelling. It's that I'm just trying to find another way.

—EDIE    *CIAO! MANHATTAN* TAPES

I want to reach people and express myself. You have to put up with the risk of being misunderstood if you are going to try to communicate. You have to put up with people projecting their own ideas, attitudes, misunderstanding you. But it's worth being a public fool if that's all you can be in order to communicate yourself.

**—EDIE**

I saw her as a free spirit, because she was an artist, you always have to remember, she was an artist, she drew, she sketched horses on her walls.

**—DANNY FIELDS**

She has artistic talent, drawing these horses that she drew. And you'd go, "Look at the spirit in that. That's her." The muscular freedom of that drawing. And in so many ways she felt like a colt, like a wild colt. So the fact that she would draw that was like, "Oh, self-portraits, interesting, great."

**—L. M. KIT CARSON**

Edie was romantic in a kind of like, almost a classical way, like an English country way, but not gushy. Her sculpture was never sentimental. If she did animals, she got the real animal.

**—CHUCK WEIN**

Edie's style was an absolutely perfect self-realization of her art form, of herself, without trying to be this or that . . . There's an eternal quality to that look that she created. She painted her eyelids with watercolor.

**—BIBBE HANSEN**

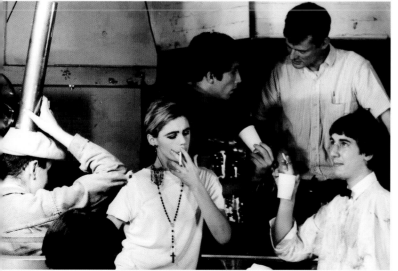

"She wanted to learn things, she picked up things, she was a vibration and she would pick up on the vibrations, and the meanings of things."

—DONALD LYONS

It's balletic; it was a magic kind of thing. She expected everyone else to be wonderful, by nature. It wasn't like a pretense, or you're supposed to be wonderful with Edie, it was more like her attitude was, "Everyone I meet in the world is going to be absolutely wonderful, and we're all going to have a beautiful, smooth, wonderful time." She was on a little cloud all the time, holding on to a lightning bolt. She welcomed everyone that way, and if you weren't that way, in a sense she was disappointed . . . But she . . . took it in stride, as if that's what the world is like and maybe we don't put our wings on today.

—BILLY NAME

The two of us, over the time we knew each other, exchanged parts of a story, the adventures of a strange golden creature that the two of us would write chapters on . . . It was the story of a golden girl escaping from the green giants, and so forth, that were out to capture and devour her, and what she wore, and so forth. It was a half-silly adventure story.

—DONALD LYONS

The colors . . . oh, I see the most fantastic things. Do you realize when people just close their eyes what they see? It's unbelievable. Colors and things, forms of every sort. I wonder if that happens for everybody?

**—EDIE**
***INNER AND OUTER SPACE***

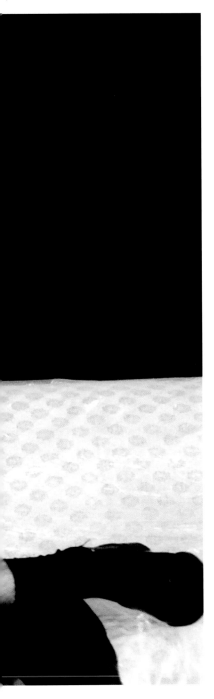

I gave her a history of the ancient world. I don't think I actually read it myself, but I think she did. She was incredibly absorbing and retentive, and it all came fresh to her. It had no context, ancient Iraq or Rome, you know, it might have been last week in New Jersey, but it had the force of a life she didn't know. You got the impression that the creature, that Edie, was made literally by Zeus three weeks ago, that there was no past to her, save what she picked up from books and people. With her there was no traditional structure, no formal structure. She indeed would compare Raymond Chandler or Jane Austen or ancient Rome to what she experienced last night with the tuna fish, but it was marvelous and fresh.

**—DONALD LYONS**

I came to New York to see what I could see—that's from a children's book, isn't it?—and to find the living part.

**—EDIE**

# FAIRY TALE

That is unusual, to look like you had just walked out of a fairy tale. She had nothing human about her, just mystery.

**—IVY NICHOLSON**

I think Edie's creation of her persona, of her image, was her art form.

**—BIBBE HANSEN**

Saints are always vulnerable, because they are sacrificial, so I suppose there was that implicit in her, that she was sacrificial. She was so extremely magical that she was evanescent. She was there and not there at the same time.

**—L. M. KIT CARSON**

I lived a very isolated life. When you start at 20, you have a lot of nonsense to work out of your system.

**—EDIE**

It's childlike in one sense. You're going in somewhere that's forbidden, in the sense that you're being invited into somewhere that's kind of mysterious and special.

—JOHN PALMER

This is about Edie, and she's the most elusive and the most difficult to capture, and I was in her presence masses of times, but I'm left with a visceral impression, not a vocal one that I can communicate because she changed lives of anyone she knew back then with her shimmering presence. It is like taking something ineffable. You know, Tinkerbell is always represented just by a light on stage and a little tympani in the orchestra. There's no person there. It's just a little baby spot that goes around.

—RENE RICARD

I talked about her living in the film frame. I think she was very much playing make-believe as a child.

—BIBBE HANSEN

# THE FACTORY

The Factory was the great electro-magnet at the center of all these runaways or displaced people, or people going through a generational change.

**—DANNY FIELDS**

The Silver Factory was like being inside a silver-lined box. It was fascinating.

**—IVY NICHOLSON**

All those runaway kids landed in the Factory, and so the door was open. That was Warhol's contribution to delinquency, that there was a door open and you could land there, and you could be accepted there.

**—ULTRA VIOLET**

I never went there. I think they were confusing talent with decadence.

**—BARTLE BULL**

I remember Andy sitting on the couch, smoking, and people would come over and go down on one knee and say, "Shall I shoot this from over here?" And he'd go, "Yes." And they'd go away again. It was like a royal court. It was his fiefdom, just as the ranch had been her father's, and everyone there served to bear him up. I think it must have felt very familiar for her.

**—ROBIN SEDGWICK**

The Factory was very much like a European court . . . It was everyone for themselves, and no one knew what the other one was doing because everyone was very jealous of their role . . . I think a court is like that, where each person is their own state, two people are a cabal, and three people are a conspiracy!

**—RENE RICARD**

The whole space was silvery, painted silver, aluminum, even the windows. You also had on the ceiling a mirror ball, like in the discothèque, and it functioned like a gigantic mirror, and we could look in the mirror all the time and see who we were or who we wanted to be.

**—ULTRA VIOLET**

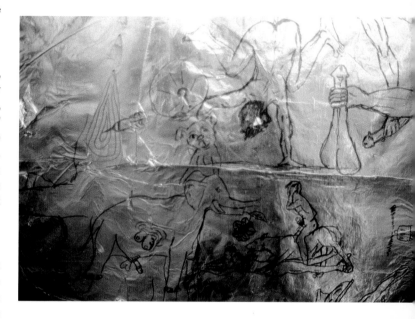

A yin and a yang, if you want to put it that way. It was great in that there was a totally permissive quality to [the Factory], and theoretically you could do any damn thing you wanted to. Although there was something quite tyrannical about Andy, so on the other hand there was a quality of exploitation that bordered on the sadistic sometimes.

—FRED EBERSTADT

And Andy said, "What do you think of Edie?" And I said, "Oh, she looks like a downtown poetess!" And he liked that, and he said, "Really?" And I said, "Yes, she's rather piquant looking!" And he says, "Piquant?" and I said, "Yes, P-I-Q-U-A-N-T." And he says, "What does that mean?"

—RENE RICARD

*Piquant* adj 1: having an agreeably pungent taste [syn: savory, savoury, spicy, zesty] 2: engagingly stimulating or provocative; "a piquant wit"; "salty language" [syn: salty] 3: attracting or delighting; "an engaging frankness"; "a piquant face with large appealing eyes" [syn: engaging]

The fact that this new world, in the bowels of New York, was mostly homosexual may have been a relief for her, and an escape from the invasively sexual aura of the ranch.

—ROBIN SEDGWICK

**I was kind of turned off for the time being, going out with men, because I was very upset that two of my brothers had committed suicide, two that I love very much. It kinda screwed up my head, so I just freaked out for a while.**

**—EDIE**

Description of Factory: Fun, interesting, and fabulous.

—JANE HOLZER

It was what was happening. You could go back home and say, "We went to the Factory." Everyone would, you know, "Oh my god, you were there?!"

—ROBIN SEDGWICK

I landed in that Factory, and I heard the voice of Andy, that very odd voice, almost like a ventriloquist. You had the feeling you had to put a coin into his mouth so he would say something.

**—ULTRA VIOLET**

The Factory people to me were the scum of American society. A bunch of rich kids who could get away with it simply because they were rich kids.

**—NAT FINKELSTEIN**

The Factory was like a launching pad; you felt it happening. It was like a locus.

**—RENE RICARD**

There were a lot of people around the Factory who were on a very fine edge . . . and that's what I didn't like about it. Although I'm a shrink, I don't like crazy people.

**—FRED EBERSTADT**

For a quotidian kind of maverick debutante from the West to be doing this in this Tinsel Factory, with all these people on speed, listening to Dionne Warwick and Burt Bacharach, she's a real idol.

**—JOHN PALMER**

The Factory was very interesting in that Andy did attract every kind of person. I'm sure there were criminals, but on the other hand there were bankers and Salvador Dalí and movie stars and heads of state. It was a real crossroads, and it was very entertaining.

**—FRED EBERSTADT**

The thing about Andy Warhol's Factory, though, was that I never thought it was a descent into the lower depths. It was a halfway house.

**— GEORGE PLIMPTON**

And Edie, in there, just going on and people saying she's been doing this, you know, for three hours ... She'd sit on a table and talk and sort of do stuff and laugh. I don't know, I guess it was my first real view of performance art, and I guess what I had seen a year or two ago at the [Fishers Island] party was kind of a personal rehearsal, you know ... Maybe she became aware of how it rather fascinated and attracted people and ended up, you know, doing it for the camera, with people more scripting it.

—ROBIN SEDGWICK

PERFORMANCE

I think that she was a bit brave in the
way that she was a bit fearless to be
in those movies . . . Looking back at
me looking at it then—we're getting
very Proustian here—she had the
most amazing and wonderful quality
to live in the film frame. To live there,
to breathe, to inhabit it.

**—BIBBE HANSEN**

To play the poor little rich girl in this movie, Edie didn't need a script—if she needed a script, she wouldn't have been right for the part.

—ANDY WARHOL, *POPism*

We call what we are doing *synscintima*—"syn" for synthetic, "scin" for scintillating, and "intima" for the personal nature or intimate nature of the films. We have dubbed the whole thing "reel-real," or the idea of the reel of film creating the reality.

—CHUCK WEIN

Donald and I used to chase people down the street who were really cute and say, "Do you want to be in a movie?"

—DANNY FIELDS

When she was doing these experiments with Chuck Wein, she was just being interviewed the way I am. That's all Chuck's idea was, to interview her off camera. I don't think they had much idea what to do with her.

—PAUL MORRISSEY

**If all I cared about was me, I could make a million. And that's what they will never understand.**

**—EDIE**

**EDIE:** . . . everybody and their real selves by just taking a close-up shot . . . How can you fit in, like you can fit in Ondine and Don-Don maybe, but when it gets to be more than that they'll lose their real—

**ANDY:** Yeah, but, I mean he'll know it's a role—

**EDIE:** I mean, what is your concern, just a nothing?

**ANDY:** No, but—

**EDIE:** Like, just a bunch of people? Who cares?

**ANDY:** No, no, no, no I mean that.

**EDIE:** You have fabulous people there, do you want to take advantage of them?

**ANDY:** If, uh . . . well then we can't have Don and Eddy there tomorrow.

**EDIE:** Yes you can. You have three reels.

**ANDY:** Then it's like three different movies. They'll be like coming in in each reel.

**EDIE:** That isn't the point. The point is, what are you going to make of it on film.

**ANDY:** I was going to have—

**EDIE:** I mean what *might* happen is a thousand possibilities.

**ANDY:** Ondine'll just work with you at the beginning, and then uh—

**EDIE:** Oh, you mean just—

**ANDY:** —won't even pay any attention to Don-O at all.

**EDIE:** And Don-O will be there, and then you change . . .

**ANDY:** Yeah.

**EDIE:** Hmm.

**FACTORY TAPE OF ANDY AND EDIE
DISCUSSING PLANS FOR THE NEXT
DAY'S FILMING**

You know, Andy as director didn't exist. Andy turned on the lights or had Gerard or Paul turn them on. He thought that the setting was amusing or viable, and let people carry on as they willed.

—DONALD LYONS

All the movies with Edie were so innocent that when I think back on them, they had more of a pajama-party atmosphere than anything else.

—ANDY WARHOL, *POPism*

They adored each other. At first they were very close. They grew apart in time, as we all did. Like a director of a movie, you know, when the movie was over, when Andy decided to concentrate on x, y, or z, he moved on.

**—DONALD LYONS**

# YOU LIVE ALONE,
creating your life as you go.

**—EDIE**

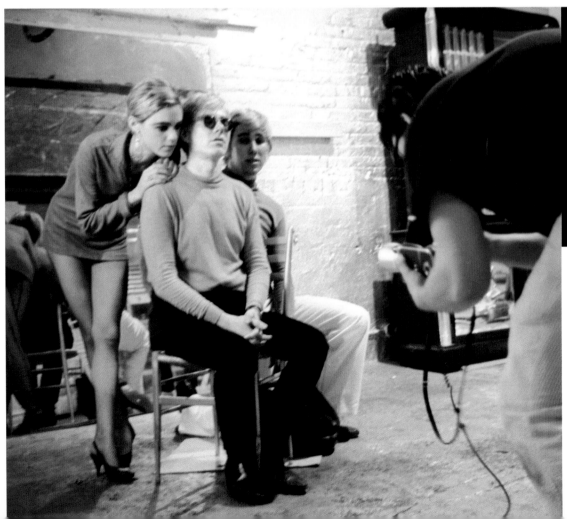

Edie & Andy

Edie was his greatest creation, because he was about self-manufacture; Edie was his greatest doppelganger.

—RENE RICARD

Edie went with the Factory, went with Andy very easily: dressed like Andy for a while, became the consort of Andy, became the girl Andy.

—DONALD LYONS

This is what makes you crazy, the strength of her soul. The Warhol thing was like, they were lucky, that's all. They didn't create her.

—L. M. KIT CARSON

There was a romance between the two, one of two artists, almost like two collaborationists.

—BIBBE HANSEN

[Edie and Andy] had fun. They egged each other on, and I think Edie carried Andy into some kinds of situations. I mean, she wasn't his passport, because he was the one who had been invited, or they had been invited together, but it was nearly gleeful some of the time. I think they really had a good time for a while.

—GORDON BALDWIN

She saw through what he was doing, or what he was trying to use her for. Andy—there was a certain amount of resentment. Andy saw her as the "have" . . .

—CHUCK WEIN

ANDY: Come on, camp it up Ondine.
EDIE: Oh, camp it up yourself.

*AFTERNOON*

I wonder how close he ever got to her, though. She never threw her arms around him. No, they were more like a sister and brother team, I think.

—IVY NICHOLSON

I was not enthusiastic about it, in the sense it was none of my business. But on the other hand I thought at first it was exploitive on Andy's part, and then I changed my mind, and decided if it was exploitive on any part, maybe it was exploitive on Edie's part. Then I thought, well, what the hell, they're two publicity-seekers, attention-seekers, and I guess they're binding up each other's wounds.

—FRED EBERSTADT

**I act this way because that's the way I feel like acting. If people like it—fine. If they don't, that's their problem.**

**—EDIE**

Andy was very kind to Edie, and to everybody. He never promised more than he could deliver. He was a film director and a photographer. He didn't promise a life to these people, he promised just the afternoon to them. Andy, insofar as he had a coherent philosophy, which is not very far, believed in seeing everybody and letting everybody run amok, in filming them destroying themselves, and he didn't care. He was willing to be kind, but that was as far as it went.

—DONALD LYONS

Andy didn't quite develop relationships with people, except with Edie . . . He liked people who were sort of vulnerable and needed help. He was so lame himself, and to him everybody was sort of better off than he was. So when he found a sort of lost soul, he sort of took a little interest, and I think he did that with Edie.

—PAUL MORRISSEY

I think Andy absolutely adored her.

—JANE HOLZER

Edie and Andy were into this kind of
Bobbsey-twin alter-ego thing.

**—BIBBE HANSEN**

One person in the sixties fascinated
me more than anybody I had ever
known. And the fascination I experienced was probably very close to a
certain kind of love.

**—ANDY WARHOL,**
***THE PHILOSOPHY OF WARHOL***

I think that Andy had a presence like that of a protective father, as an identity provider. This was all a construct of Edie's and of society's at the time, of course. It was very unreal, and everyone knew it was unreal, and so did Edie. I don't think Andy pretended to be anything he wasn't. He pretended to be a "let's go to the party this afternoon, wear that, don't wear that, cut your hair this way . . ." So Edie is his latest demonstration. She was delighted and amused to be the—fashion model is too weak a word for it—the creature of Andy. But I don't think she took it for more than it was, and I don't think Andy did, but there was no tomorrow for Edie.

**—DONALD LYONS**

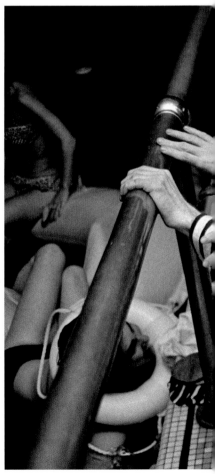

The essential thing about the whole Warhol world, and the reason I got out of it . . . *had* to get out of it to save myself, is that Andy's a voyeur, and he needs exhibitionists around . . . which is all right. But he's also kind of a sadist. He's a voyeur-sadist, and he needs exhibitionist-masochists in order to fulfill both halves of his destiny. And it's obvious that an exhibitionist-masochist is not going to last very long. You know, you go up in a fine burst of flames, and then you die out. And then the voyeur-sadist needs another exhibitionist-masochist.

—HENRY GELDZAHLER

Sort of like a sandbox, with a bunch of aristocrats in the sandbox. She was in the sandbox with Andy.

—JOHN PALMER

I think Edie blamed Andy for her own mistakes. I think we all blamed Andy for our own mistakes. Andy had that kind of vacuum, that you could read things in, that was his public persona, but that was a big part of Andy . . . Andy's passivity was a Zen tactic that he used, that became himself.

—RENE RICARD

happening to you. I hope this letter finds you well on the way to recovery and with it I send you *all* my love.

Bundles of hugs and kisses,
♡ Edie ☺

EDITH M. SEDGWICK
722 WEST 168ᵀᴴ St.
NEW YORK
NEW YORK 10032

Beatrix Potter's original illustration for
*The Tale of Two Bad Mice*

© FREDERICK WARNE & CO LTD, LONDON & NEW YORK

*June 4ᵗʰ, 1968*

Darling Andy,
I was horribly upset to hear how you were severely injured. I am With All Good Wishes saying prayers for you --- don't know how much good they do, but at least you will know I care, and care tremendously.

You are one of the few people who really matter to me, and I can't bear the thought of anything bad

# The Beach

**EDIE:** It was heaven . . . we went out to the beach after we had a two-hour breakfast at some tacky little diner . . . and then we went out . . . we didn't realize what we looked like, but all of a sudden there we were with two enormous, bug-eaten fur coats, two black umbrellas . . . This is out on the beach in the middle of nowhere . . . I just I suddenly discovered that there we were, walking down the beach, stretches of white sand, and three little people, marching with furs and umbrellas . . . and my plastic make-up bag . . . *(laughs)* Chuck and . . . um . . . Drella? *(laughs)* . . .

I was the only one that went in swimming . . . the waves at that time were coming in really quite strong . . . and there was a big undertow . . . I had a fabulous time, and nobody else could go in, and Chuck got out and said, "Oh, wow . . .

I mean, this is not . . . this is ridiculous . . . it's ice . . . it's ice . . . and I am swimming around the water, and Chuck decided he'd come in . . . tore off down the beach . . . Oh, it was so great . . .

**ARTHUR LOEB:** Isn't that just like love?

**EDIE:** No, it wasn't . . . that's the point . . . it wasn't at all . . . but, anyway, nobody else would go in . . . Chuck wouldn't . . .

**ARTHUR LOEB:** I'm just saying if worse comes to worst . . . you could always, you know, make a fortune of . . .

**EDIE:** Going into the sea?

***AFTERNOON***

# PHOTOGRAPHING Edie: BURT GLINN

Burt Glinn's photographs of Edie, Chuck, and Andy in the manhole were taken on January 1, 1966, for an article in the London newspaper *The Sunday Times*. ★

I was going to meet Andy, and I went down to the street, and for a while nobody came, and then he showed up with Edie and Chuck Wein. But I didn't know that they were going to be in the picture . . . Edie sort of took it over, you know?

She had the brights and the smarts and the instinct . . . She was going to sit on the ground and lean against it [a manhole], and put her legs up in the air. I don't want to take credit for any kind of creativity on that . . . She kind of took over the whole session because Andy didn't say a word.

I didn't think of her as a great beauty. I thought of her as a kind of vivacious and lively woman . . . I think she was attractive, but the thing that made her better is that she made a room kind of come alive when she came in it because, you know, she and Andy used to go to parties kind of as a prop for a party. A party was considered a success if Andy Warhol and Edie Sedgwick came in. Well, when they came in Andy sort of . . . you never saw him at all after that, unless he was taking pictures with his Polaroid camera. Edie was the one that gobbled up the room with her energy.

She really, as somebody said, she really could say hello.

When she was with Andy, she reminded me of a Scott Fitzgerald lady, you know? She was alive, and she was able to put a party aspect on everything . . . So when we did this picture . . . She lit that thing up. She made it a picture, she made it an occasion.

It was her spirit that set that shot up.

—BURT GLINN

She gave to me the impression of being born just before we met her, and a raging, furious desire to assimilate as much of life as she could.

**—DONALD LYONS**

JOY

The real Edie is where the action is. Fast cars, fast horses, and people doing things!

**—EDIE**

It's not that she wanted the next party. She wanted the next joy. She wanted the next sense of fun. That was the feeling that she gave.

—DONALD LYONS

I think she had a naiveté. That's how she was able to dominate . . . because she had no self-judgment, except on this *deep* level.

—L. M. KIT CARSON

She made you feel privileged to be there.

—RENE RICARD

It's an attitude. I mean you can feel it, you can feel a person's intelligence when you're around, when you're looking around the room, you both can see and . . . connect. It's unspoken. There's an amusement that she had. She was not impressed. *Pff!* That's good. See, those are all marks of intelligence.

—L. M. KIT CARSON

We enjoyed ourselves most by going to parties. Entering the door was like going on stage.

—ED HENNESSEY

I think that she was inclusive, which is one of the reasons that she's a revolutionary. You get the sense that she's willing to jump across boundaries and barriers and so on. And that she's looking at people as people.

**—JOHN PALMER**

She thought it was funny that people thought they were important.

**—L. M. KIT CARSON**

Often, the funniest things she said were inadvertent, like asking Salvador Dalí what it was like being a famous writer. In retrospect, I wonder if she knew *exactly* who he was and wanted to tease him. In any event, he roared with laughter.

**—ED HENNESSEY**

**EDIE**: In the year 2000 you're going to have a problem . . . Leisure time will be a problem in the year 2000 . . . I just want you to realize . . . I just want to make sure that you know of it now . . .

***SPACE***

Her looks, her expressions, I think, were her sense of humor.

**—JANE HOLZER**

It wasn't a normal sense of humor. It wasn't the thing, like, jokes. It was like, she loved situations. She thought Ondine and Eddie Hennessey were a scream . . . She admired the people who could cut loose and not care what the world thought of them.

—CHUCK WEIN

Life was a perpetual dance party . . . The great temptation about the Factory was that it was a perpetual party in one place or another. So that there was an opportunity to end-lessly experience the sense of life as a joy.

—DONALD LYONS

I'm afraid of habit patterns . . . It would be too much of a routine if you had to establish definite ways of getting through things. You'd get very bored.

—EDIE

ARTHUR: What are your plans for marriage?

EDIE: I'm, there's only, you know I can only marry one of four, three people.

ARTHUR: Who?

EDIE: The first . . . and foremost, which might have to be the last, and uh, Mick Jagger . . .

**UNTITLED WARHOL TAPE**

**I'd have to believe in it to get started. And uh, so, just right away, I can't fake it, you know? Like, I can't marry somebody like, say Francois were a little more straightened out. I couldn't marry him without knowing exactly what I was doing. You know? 'Cause I'm too removed in one sense not to realize how my life runs according to Francois' general background and how mine should run according to my general background. I mean I am a freak in that sense. It does make you a freak. But at the same time, it's a true thing. It's not; it's seeing actualities and true relationships and it's caring. It's all things that people wish about other people, either in a true way or a fake way.**

**—EDIE**

# MARRIAGE?

I believe the last time I saw her and we really spoke was at my birthday party, 1965, and she was now in her twin stage with Andy . . . They came in identical short white-blond haircuts and as much of the same gear as possible and both very sort of thin and high-strung and more comfortable as the evening darkened, if you know what I mean . . . It was a very crowded party on Riverside Drive. In fact, Jackie came, a lot of other people. It was a very bizarre evening, all kinds of people, and that was the last time that Edie and I really had a talk. We did go off and chat there, but she struck me as very shaky and as on a bit of a tightrope. I think it was just the beginning of her getting too much under Andy's control, and with that neurotic rule of drugs and all the rest.

And after that I never really saw her to speak with her, you know, maybe the occasional large party or something like that . . . By the time I saw her at my birthday party with Andy, I could see that she had succumbed to her weakness of sort of adapting to the drama of the moment and that sort of powerful aura of Andy's culture and excitement and drugs and all that stuff was beginning to lure her, and she was getting into it and surrendering to it. I thought she was on a dangerous path. I think it had ups and downs . . . at dramatic social moments, she would appear lively and giddy, and then . . . probably got a bit more morbid on those down swings. But that's just an impression. It wasn't my experience with her, because I wasn't with her through those horrific adventures. But I think, though, the people that she was hanging around with have a moral burden for what happened to her and also for the general corruption they spread by making young people think that decadent self-destructive behavior was charming. So I think they have quite a lot to answer for.

—BARTLE BULL

## BARTLE BULL'S BIRTHDAY

Bartle Bull had a birthday party in spring 1965 on New York's Upper West Side to which he invited Edie, who arrived with Andy dressed identically. ★

**DONALD LYONS:** I think you just wanna be the person who gets the moon.

**EDIE:** I'm already half there . . . and I didn't choose it either.

**DANGER.**

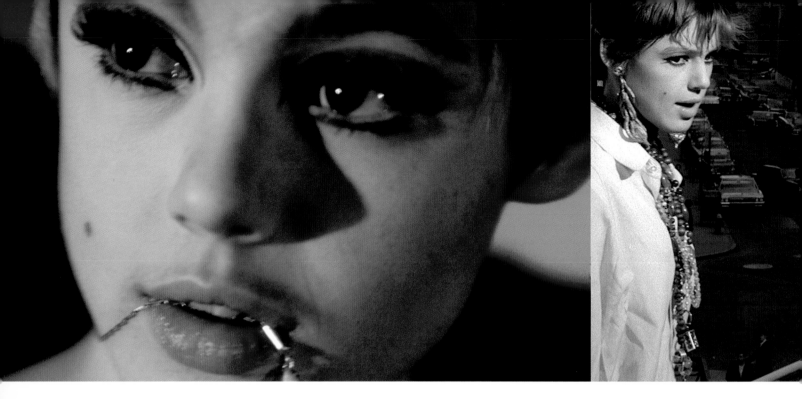

Edie was always someone who seemed in danger . . . There was this sanctity of vulnerability that she had, this "I'm a clown, I'm a beautiful clown," then your heart was right there going, "Okay, I'm going to make sure everything's okay here." At the same time, she was so powerful that you didn't have to make sure everything was okay, but it was okay for you to try to keep your eyes open for what she was going through, what she was putting herself into. There's an out-of-control thing about her.

—L. M. KIT CARSON

EDIE ON MONITOR: . . . Somehow I believe in the magical sense of things . . . Do you think I could have a cigarette? . . . EDIE WATCHING HERSELF: Isn't that sad! I'm so fragile. It's tragic *[laugh]*. Can you believe it? That's so sad.

**INNER AND OUTER SPACE**

And then you'd look at that and see this flash, and then in retrospect you'd see this shadow right behind the flash. And that's why the flash stands out so much.

—L. M. KIT CARSON

The craziest thing I ever saw Edie do was an arabesque.

—JANE HOLZER

When you'd see her with a straight man, it was always as if she was on a wild ride, and didn't know where she was going to land.

—RENE RICARD

You couldn't know Edie without knowing she was vulnerable and probably fragile. In a sense, the danger was part of her charm.

—FRED EBERSTADT

Edie saw herself as tough like a little tomboy.

—CHUCK WEIN

[People] weren't leading her by a ring in her nose, and she probably wasn't unwilling to take certain steps, but she had an incompleteness and a vulnerability that I think a lot of people took advantage of, after she came to New York especially.

—BARTLE BULL

He said, how would I like to shoot up some acid with him, and this is really mind-blowing, [he was] a new doctor. I had never met him before. I just got his name from a friend of mine. I used to get my drugs from another gyne-cologist, but since I was committed to Gracie Square, I couldn't get any of my old connections to give me anything. I hadn't had that much experience with acid, but I had hard drug experience, and I wasn't afraid. So he closed up his office at five and we took off in his Aston Martin and drove up the coast or up the . . . I'm not sure exactly where we headed, I think it was up . . . What's the name of that river that . . . the Hudson, yeah, and we stopped at a motel, and he gave me three ampules intravenously, mainlining, and he gave himself the same amount, and he completely flipped. I was hallucinating and explaining to him, you know, I'd say, I see rich, embroidered curtains and I see people moving in the background. But I realized I was hallucinating. He believed we were in the Middle Ages, and that I was some kind of a princess, and he was some sort of royalty. And we made love from about five in the afternoon till seven in the morning with ecstatic climax after climax, and just going insane until he realized . . . he had to get to his office . . . He gave me a shot to calm me down, and I took about fourteen Placidil, 'cause I was so stoned I couldn't come down. I was afraid I had overdone it, and on the way back he straightened out very well, and I just . . . something very strange happened. I didn't realize I was going to say it, and I said, out loud, "I wish I was dead." And the reason I said it was the love and the beauty and the ecstasy of the whole experience was really an alien experience in a way, because I didn't even know him. It was a one-night jag. He was married and had children, and I just felt really, like, lost. It just wasn't worth living anymore because I was all alone again.

—EDIE

But at the same time, her neediness for nurture and feeding began to be fed in her life by the attention she got from others around her, and the drinking and the drugs and the high life. The irony, of course, being that the more she did the more she needed it, because it wasn't being built into her psyche. It was still on the outside. It was still in a way an addictive thing that didn't make her feel any more of a person when it happened.

—ROBIN SEDGWICK

It always related back to the family and the ranch because that's where most of her experience was, plus fear of what might affect her reality. You know, nothing that was happening in New York, no matter how interesting it was, or good for her, wiped that out. In other words, the idea that she had to worry about being locked up was more important than being in *Vogue*. She'd put her all into it, and she would do it, and, she did it, and she just was herself in it, but she didn't care. It was still back there. What they could do to her. That was on her mind.

—CHUCK WEIN

She loved being given some sort of permission to spin about and, of course, it plays out very nicely in the rebellion against her parents.

—GORDON BALDWIN

**Then they say use it, channel it. Do it, like there will be a sign, be an artist, you're so creative, do anything, you've got to do it, use it. Then, things like, and you've gotta collect yourself, too. I mean, you know, make your hair more about yourself, self-respect. But, I mean, ridiculous. You know why my doctor got so mad this last time? He said, that scene, remember in the LSD bit, the only time I had it in that, sleeping with what's-his-name and having that sex bit go on while, it was very strange-mannered, but I certainly wasn't mortified. I mean, I humanly might be a little mortified knowing that a thousand other human beings would think it mortifying, but basically, me. So he thought that was a total lack of self-respect, which is wrong. Totally wrong.**

**—EDIE**

Edie was promiscuous at times. She had this Scorpio moon, sensual side that had nothing to do with relating to anybody. It was inner space . . . a sensual reality that's self-contained.

—CHUCK WEIN

I remember her at some, something, and she had these scars and she had, you know, made them up to make a thing of them. I thought that was kind of a great approach to life, you know, to do that.

—CHASE MELLEN

I'm not sure she saw herself because she hadn't internalized the early kind of self-soothing that we learn from having others soothe us and be gentle and caring as children. Once we build that in, we can do it for ourselves later, but she never built that in.

—ROBIN SEDGWICK

Iconic, as if she was some sort of figure . . . Madonna, Mary. It was as if she was some kind of an icon in that sense, and that all of that was going to explode, and she's acting out through all of that, about to fall off the altar and go into a thousand pieces.

—JOHN PALMER

Absolutely, staggeringly beautiful; you wanted to help her in any way you could. She had that quality. Drew upon your sympathies.

—GEORGE PLIMPTON

**EDIE:** Ondine, every time I pick up this glass I spill it.
**ONDINE:** Maybe the liquid doesn't want to be contained.
**EDIE:** Do you think it means anything?
**ONDINE:** Maybe it wants freedom.
**EDIE:** Maybe it means I shouldn't have any more . . .

***AFTERNOON***

You knew that you couldn't really have her, everybody knew that, that she was doomed. You just knew that.

—DANNY FIELDS

There was this club called Ondine, it was on 59th Street, under the 59th Street bridge . . . this was before Max's . . . this was the beginning of a mixture of society with artists, money, no money, blah, blah, blah. Some nights you could see Tennessee Williams at a table, and Jim Morrison all in leather against the walls, and then another night would have Diana Ross and the Supremes. It was before they were really known, singing two feet away from you in little black dresses, and so it was quite a place. One night I was there and, although I always looked terribly sophisticated and sure of myself, I was a mess inside and incredibly shy. I was wearing my little black sophisticated dresses and high-heel shoes. I went to the bathroom, and there I saw the most incredible creature I have ever seen, and it was this young woman with alabaster skin, incredibly pale, paler than me, actually, which was difficult to do. She had short, Jean Seberg kind of platinum hair, and the shortest, shortest, shortest garment I've ever seen on anybody ever, also white. It was barely covering her derriere and devant . . . and white. I don't know, I guess she was not wearing stockings and white shoes . . . So I was looking at this creature, and then I went to the mirror to fix my false eyelashes 'cause in those days you wore them on top, on the bottom, one-by-one, they used to fall down. So I'm fixing my eyelashes, and I see her in the mirror with an eyeliner pencil, painting a scar on her forehead in black with cross-stitches. I wasn't sure that maybe she had a scar already and she was just exaggerating it or it was just some trick. I don't know what it meant, but I was terrified. So the evening went on and on and on, and then it's like so late. Almost everybody was gone, and this young man who also had platinum hair, was wearing a white suit, white shoes, a white t-shirt, I think, or shirt, I think his name was Chuck Wein, and he came over to me and he said would you like a ride home. And I was, like, scared, you know. What are those people gonna do to me? But I was so shy. I was even more scared to say no because that would've been an insult, so I said okay. We came out in a, like, glaring sunlight. It was, like, six in the morning, must have been summer, I guess, because we were not wearing coats. And they took me to the car, and it was a white Rolls-Royce. So there I was with two people totally in white, in a white Rolls-Royce, and I guess they were quite charming because nothing happened to me that I remember, exactly. So that was my first impression of Edie Sedgwick, which was quite strong on my shy persona.

—LARISSA

It was estimable in some ways, you know, that she was just living her life in such a free way. I mean, not many people are so free.

—CHASE MELLEN

Why would someone surround themselves with homosexuals? And only feel safe with homosexuals?

—RENE RICARD

She would do almost anything that came into her head.

—L. M. KIT CARSON

**Stripped off all my clothes, leapt downstairs, and ran two blocks down Park Avenue before my friends caught me. Naked. Naked as a lima bean.**

**—EDIE**

EDIE: That was a dream? . . . It's like my having to walk down thousands and thousands of white marble stairs . . . and nothing but very, very blue sky, very blue like . . . Yes, and I'd have to walk down them forever. I never thought about going up . . . I don't know, don't you think that must mean something? It never occurred to me to turn it around. I mean, why didn't I think that way? This was after I had the car accident . . . I don't know. I think I've run out of time.

***POOR LITTLE RICH GIRL***

She was clearly a needful person. I mean, that wasn't an act. She was, and the signs of self-destructiveness and the shattering were there for everyone to see from the beginning, from the Mercedes that she crashed while driving on acid to the fires that she started.

—DANNY FIELDS

EDIE: I'm out of my mind! Somebody told me that a long time ago. Some idiot! [laugh] . . . in a dream. I don't want to think about dreams now.

***INNER AND OUTER SPACE***

Judy Garland was definitely there. David Whitney danced by in the arms of Rudolf Nureyev. Edie looked beautiful that night, laughing a lot with Brian Jones. Juliet Prowse, who'd just broken up with Frank Sinatra. Tennessee Williams. Allen Ginsberg and William Burroughs. Montgomery Clift. The stars went out and the superstars came in. There were more people staring at Edie than at Judy. But to me Edie and Judy had something in common—a way of getting everyone totally involved in their problems. When you were around them, you forgot you had problems of your own, you got so involved in theirs. They had dramas going 'round the clock, and everybody loved to help them through it all. Their problems made them even more attractive.

—ANDY WARHOL, *POPism*

**EDIE:** I say the word death a lot . . . think of it as . . . primal relations, opposite, so if I say death a lot, it means I'm concerned with life. It's true.

***INNER AND OUTER SPACE***

## I need to dance it out.

**—EDIE**

She was wonderful to watch . . . When she couldn't think of anything else to do she danced. She would kind of dance across the room. She danced all the time.

**—FRED EBERSTADT**

Life was something you danced out in the afternoon, something you danced out in the evening . . .

**—DONALD LYONS**

Music always got her into her own world. She loved to put on music and do her own little dance. She could do her own act, which was very spellbinding. The movements she made weren't rock and roll; they were just Edie. Edie to whatever beat there was.

**—CHUCK WEIN**

She would do these sort of pirouettes with one leg raised, and it was like no one else's dancing, and her hands would somehow disconnect at the wrist, so it was a little bit like a praying mantis in a way. Just the way she looked when she moved.

**—GORDON BALDWIN**

Her dance moves were sort of Egyptian, with her head and chin tilting in just the right, beautiful way. People called it the Sedgwick, and Edie was the only one who did it—everybody else was doing the jerk.

**—ANDY WARHOL, POPism**

To Edie, money was like play money. She would blithely spend $500 for a set of false eyelashes at Bonavita, and she would be equally blithe spending $500 of her money (well, her father's money) for a luncheon party at the Ritz.

—ED HENNESSEY

MONEY

Andy's whole life was one endless photo opportunity. He couldn't go out by himself, and when he had Edie he started to get real photo opportunities. She was good for that, and also, people don't quite realize it, she almost always picked up the check for Andy.

**—PAUL MORRISSEY**

God, what she would steal . . . I would have to search her. I didn't have to, but after a while there so many little tchotchkes gone missing, it was like a frisk in an airport.

**—DANNY FIELDS**

**I lost all my jewels, including a $20,000 star sapphire.**

**—EDIE**

She showed me an after-hours bootlegger where you could get Chateau Marmont. Seriously. She knew where to get caviar. She knew where to get the most expensive anything after hours.

**—NAT FINKELSTEIN**

If she liked something, she'd buy two of them in every color.

**—CHUCK WEIN**

This doesn't interfere with the shopping, however. Money as cash didn't exist for her as a concept . . . it was, "My mother will come to New York and buy me an apartment and a leather rhinoceros from Abercrombie & Fitch."

**–DANNY FIELDS**

**CHUCK:** If you're so dead broke, how the hell did you happen to get that coat?

**EDIE:** This crazy person gave it to me. No, no, it was that funny Englishman. The one who said he was gonna give me money for the rest of my life. With nothing . . . no . . .

**CHUCK:** No strings attached.

**EDIE:** Yeah. Well, he was so crazy. I mean, what would you do if somebody came up to you and gave you a leopard coat? That's what I did.

***POOR LITTLE RICH GIRL***

You looked on Edie as someone from a family whose, like, the mother was Union Pacific, she was filthy rich, but the father had nothing. The father married the mother so [Edie] wasn't gonna run out of money, she wasn't going to be a pauper, but at the same time she never was going to control any money where she could really do anything herself—buy a house—but she'd get taken care of. The car, this and that, she could charge everything. She could go to the health food store and charge; the bill went to the grandmother. She'd order up 12 sandwiches at the deli, but the money, really, there was never really any cash around. There wasn't any. When the press were around, she'd always pick up the check. Andy would pick up the check sometimes.

—CHUCK WEIN

Her solution to the problem was very odd and very expensive. She would order three or four entirely different dishes, all at full price. When they arrived, she would sample them and eat the one she liked best. Then she would visit the ladies' room and throw up. After that she would return to the table and eat another of the meals, and so on.

—ED HENNESSEY

Once a month we would all go to dinner. She would take eleven or twelve to L'Aventura or the Gingerman, her favorite restaurants then, in that era, and the reason would be "Don-Don is going to help me with my bills."

—DANNY FIELDS

She had lost her Mercedes. They took it away because it had so many tickets on it. Her father wasn't paying her credit cards any more, and Ondine was being her maid.

—BILLY NAME

Eventually she'd go, "Oh this is so boring. Why do we have to do this now? The same bills are going to come next month!" And everyone would say, "Yeah! You're so right! Waiter! Let's all have a veal marsala or something!" And they'd scoop [the unpaid bills] all up and back in the envelope.

—DANNY FIELDS

I had no money. My parents closed down all credit. I couldn't get any money, and they were trying to lock me up again because I'd taken some acid and told my psychiatrist about it. I just told him what the experience was like and he jumped, and at the same time he read about Andy Warhol's "pornographic" movies in *Time*. I was in the studio a lot, so my psychiatrist got really upset and called my parents and was gonna have me put away, so I ran away to Europe with Andy and Chuck.

—EDIE

That would be the ritual, that would be paying the bills . . . You never paid them, you put them in piles. And she would say, "What is this? Shampoo? Forty-seven dollars for a bottle of shampoo?"

—DANNY FIELDS

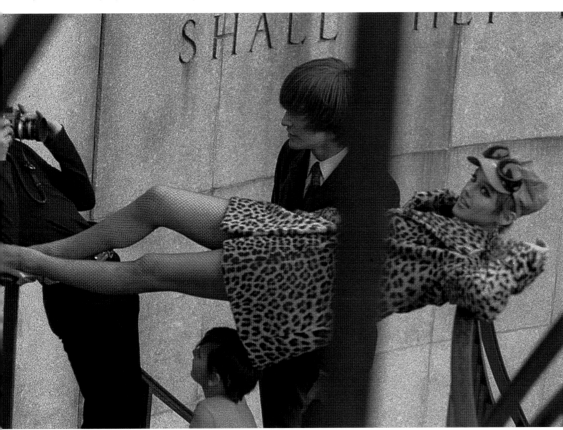

I think Edie was one of those personages. When you came in contact with her, you came away with a deep impression of her. And then she moved in circles where almost automatically with that impression came a story or some sort of an event or a happening. Everywhere she went things began to buzz and happen around her.

—GEORGE PLIMPTON

She was the girl on fire! And . . . I didn't mean it literally! I mean it figuratively. She shimmered, she shone . . . and fame has so much to do with it.

—RENE RICARD

Edie was incredible on camera—just the way she moved. And she never stopped moving for a second, even when she was sleeping, her hands were wide awake . . . The great stars are the ones who are doing something you can watch every second, even if it's just a movement inside their eye.

—ANDY WARHOL, *POPism*

She started to realize there was power in there . . . the muse.

—JOHN PALMER

I think she was discovering being famous, which is certainly one of the Ten Commandments, if not the First through the Tenth, of the Warhol mantra and philosophy. It was her time to be in the eye of fashion.

—DANNY FIELDS

She was aware of her impact, as a precursor to the red carpet. The dazzle-catcher.

—JOHN PALMER

The public was something to amuse, to amuse one's self with. They both enjoyed that sense of it, the sense of themselves as theater.

—DONALD LYONS

As the Factory, as the Warhol thing was a kind of parody of Hollywood, so our lives were meant to be parodies of, if you will, stardom. We felt that, and we didn't take ourselves seriously though.

—DONALD LYONS

That's it. It represented everything to me . . . radiating intelligence, speed, being connected with the moment.

—PATTI SMITH

FAME

Even to people in England, she was a more easily understandable pop figure. I think what she was, was to a regular girl, she represented something that they could understand in that movement. I mean, I couldn't understand Andy Warhol, I didn't understand any of those things, but I sure understood that she was gorgeous, and she was wonderful, and she was part of that big change that made everything more fun.

—JANET PALMER

When we were going to a party, she would put on her makeup in a certain way, and it was interesting because she, you know, put a mask on. But it was a kind of clown mask, a kind of beautiful clown mask . . . It is to do with how she wanted to meet people.

—L. M. KIT CARSON

As Edie got more famous, she totally changed, and the shimmer got stronger, and stronger, and stronger.

—RENE RICARD

There was this conflict, this complete contradiction. She would go dominate a room, walk into a party and dominate a whole room, and then this would be like her trying to hurt herself. So there she is, in control of reality, and then she wants to be completely out of reality.

—L. M. KIT CARSON

She seemed to move through all of these circles with such ease. Naiveté. She didn't know this person was bad. She didn't know this was a bad thing to be doing. She just had no concept of any of those possibilities, and so she just flitted through, like a moth. Beautiful moth.

—GEORGE PLIMPTON

Rene Ricard's Rule of Three: You can know somebody before they're famous, you can know someone while they're famous, and you can know somebody after they're famous, but you cannot know them all three times. So I knew Edie before she was famous, and I was making movies with her while she was famous, and then she vanished.

—RENE RICARD

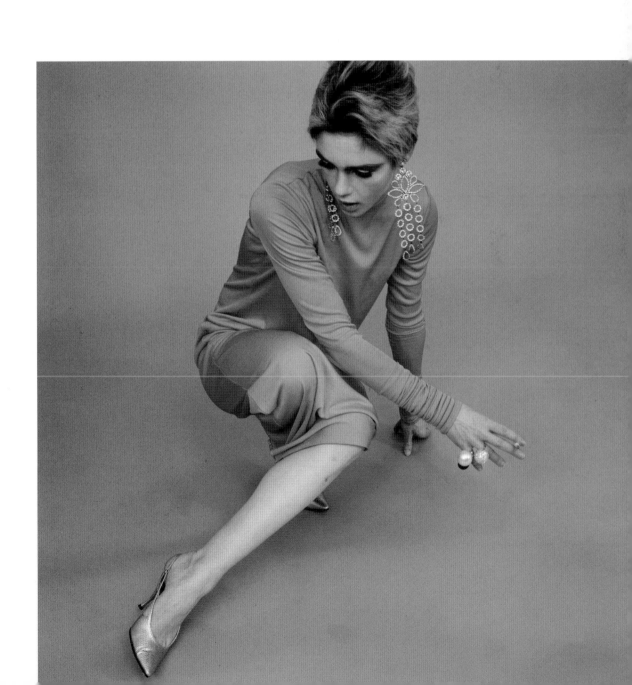

Whereever I've been, I've been quite

# notorious.

**—EDIE**

# THE MUSEUM OF MODERN ART

On April 9, 1965, Edie and Andy make one of their first public appearances together at a party at the Museum of Modern Art in New York. ★

What happened was, because we were getting so much publicity, they kept trying to tell Andy that he had to, you know, pretend like he was gonna take Edie to premieres and use us, use her, you know, her vibe, right? That thing there at the Museum of Modern Art . . . They told her that I was going to meet her there, then they never even told me that they were going. There was an opening, and Jackie Kennedy was there. They got Edie there, and then they set it up, they had the photographers and all of that, like Edie was Andy's date or something. Edie had no clue, she was just going to the gig.

**—CHUCK WEIN**

Edie was in some kind of a clingy dress, and she looked very, very fetching . . . She was standing and she said, "Do you know these people here?" And I said, "Some of them, I guess." She said, "I don't know anybody. Will you stay with me?" And I said, "Edie, what do you mean you don't know anybody? Everyone here knows who you are." It was remarkable, as if you went to the White House and the president said, "Stay with me. I don't know anybody here."

**—FRED EBERSTADT**

I understand that because I'm only half in this world, that it, it's always been a problem.

I want a further step for me . . . that's my process of development. I don't want to cut it off. I understand where it's been shut off for other people, and I understand the whole process in that order of things, but I see no way in that isn't a trap, that will let me out again without damaging too much, you know?

The very things I might have given in to, that demanded, that said, this is your life. I mean, this is your only way to survive, are the things I fought hardest to end. 'Cause I believed in something else. And, um, what makes that sane is that I can understand other people's situations in their own terms, but they still can't understand mine.

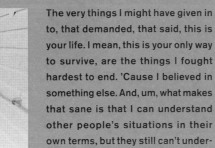

But I really, since I exist, at all, I believe that it's possible for people . . . I've lived through impossible situations. So I believe in it. I just believe, and that's the magic . . . That's the whole thing, you talk about magic that's there to believe in, and it is there. But most people don't really believe in it. And I refuse, like, since I'm still alive and done the things I've done and seen things and understood things as far as I have, and I am alive, I mean I'm physically intact. When I shouldn't be, according to medical reports and so forth. I mean I should be, not here. That's all there is to it. So the magic's working and it's a rare situation.

You care enough, that you want your life to be fulfilled in a living way, not in a painting way, not in a writing way . . . you really do want it to be involved in living, corresponding with other living objects, moving, changing, that kind of thing.

—EDIE

inner space

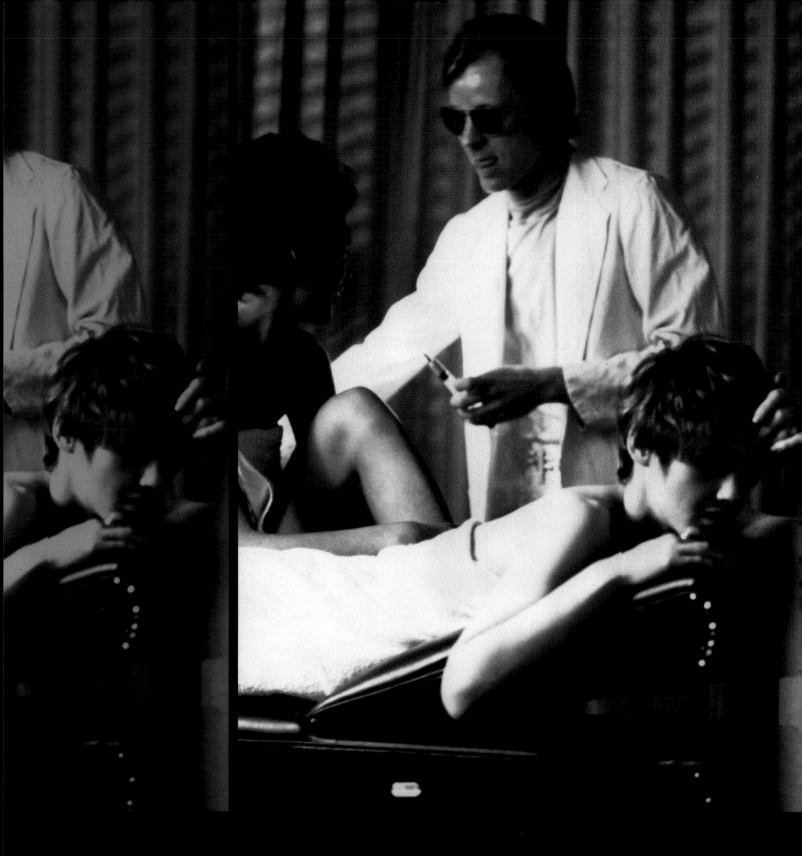

DRUGS

Susan was Andy's publicist . . . Edie was gone out of Andy's scene when Susan got in there, but . . . the other day she told me this story. She says, "The only time I met Edie is when you brought her over to my apartment, and I'll never forget going into my medicine cabinet after you guys left, and I went over to my bottle of Phenobarbital, and it was empty. There was a piece of paper in it, and I pulled it out and it said, 'Love, Edie.'" That's pretty funny. Love, Edie. Most people would, if they were really bad folks, a little fucked up, they'd just take the drugs and pretend like they didn't do it. Edie left an IOU. Love, Edie.

—SEPP DONAHOWER

That's another thing that was comfortable and familiar with the Factory for me, was that everybody did speed, and that was one of my favorite drugs.

—BIBBE HANSEN

Everyone was fascinated by it. Everyone was intrigued, and people weren't scared of it the way they maybe are now, and also, I think that it didn't seem to be that same feeling of, you know, there was no war on drugs. I just don't think people—I mean, they, obviously were against the law, but somehow . . . It wasn't as intense, and I think everyone took everything and tried everything then.

—CHASE MELLEN

**I'd like to turn the whole world on just for a moment. Just for a moment.**

**—EDIE**

EDIE: I think drugs are like strawberries and peaches.

PAUL AMERICA: I think that strong drugs allow a person to rebuild their lives, or start a new life by completely destroying the one they've been with for however many years they've been with it.

EDIE: Yeah, well, I must've tripped out a few times in a few earlier lives.

PAUL AMERICA: You think we're given more than one chance?

EDIE: Well, maybe, a whole new set of circumstances.

*CIAO! MANHATTAN* TAPES

When there were drugs, Edie was like a police dog. The Drug Enforcement Agency would have employed her to work airports. She was better than any dogs that I've seen in action. She just knew where they were, and she took them.

—DANNY FIELDS

Everybody would just be sitting there cooling their heels while she obsessed, speeding her brains out, obsessed for hours and hours and hours and hours and hours on just her eye makeup.

—BIBBE HANSEN

She would take LSD because we had all the original LSD in my refrigerator in New York. Tommy and Chucky brought it down from Leary and the erstwhile Richard Alpert, who were producing this brown liquid that you put on a sugar cube with an eyedropper . . . One drop was enough to change the life of any living human being, and there must have been thousands of drops in those bottles. And that was in my fridge.

—DANNY FIELDS

**Speed and booze, that gets funny. You get chattering at about fifty miles an hour with a downdraft and booze to kind of cool it. It can get very funny. A little ridiculous. It can go into insane ravages. It kind of gets amused somewhere between insanity and a safety zone. It's a good combination for a party. Not for an orgy though.**

**—EDIE**

Edie wasn't crazy in any way, shape or form . . . drugs would simulate madness.

—RENE RICARD

**The whole speed ravage . . . that was something I was very much a part of, but at the same time I was conked out on god knows how many Seconal and Tuinol and a lot of barbiturates to kind of cool the ravages of speed, that incredible nightmare paranoia that . . . well . . . it drives human beings crazy.**

**—EDIE**

Andy never ate, he was so high all the time. I remember seeing him once at Emilio's, where we used to go, at 4th and 6th Avenues, and he'd have to order food because, you know, everybody's eating . . . I saw him cut a black olive into 32 slices with a knife and fork.

—RENE RICARD

PAUL AMERICA: I think there's only one thing to contend with, drugs. Don't you?

EDIE: Well, there's your self and there's other people . . .

*CIAO! MANHATTAN* TAPES

**Tranquilizers, I think, do that. Put you in horizontal motion.**

**—EDIE**

# PHOTOGRAPHING EDIE: FRED EBERSTADT

Fred Eberstadt photographed Edie in the summer of 1965 for an article that never ran in *Life* magazine. ★

There was a nightclub out in Westhampton, in a barge that was moored on the beach. There was a group in there, which later became well-known, called the Monkees . . . Edie was hours late starting, and I had told the women at *Life* that was gonna happen, and they were quite nice about it, but they were really quite irritated. We all got in a couple of cars, and then Edie did this thing that alienated people enormously: She was a namedropper. She was terribly sorry, but she'd been up terribly late with Audrey Caan and Michael Caine or whoever the hell it was . . . all of which I'm sure was true, but it didn't endear her to working girls who had been up at eight o'clock that morning and maybe taken the kids to school and so forth. So we went out there and the guy who was opening the barge had been waiting for us, but that wasn't too bad because he had other things to do. But what was unfortunate is that

the band had started to practice, and Edie was all set to hang out with them . . . And I really had to be quite stern with her. Then we went out on the beach, and Edie got really into it. She began doing cartwheels and handsprings. She was very athletic . . . She had this thing where she could roll a hat up to a point, so we had a lot of fun. But, of course, the trouble is that since she was late to begin with, she began asking, "What time is it? What time is it? What time is it?" She had to get back in to have dinner with Audrey Caan and Michael Caine and whoever the hell else it was, which didn't sit too well. And that, I think, is part of the reason the stuff got killed. I felt that she was too intimidated to put everything she had into the sitting. She had to keep this celebrity life going at the same time, so there was kind of a real confusion about what was going on there.

The word *professional* jars, because she wasn't professional. That was, in a sense, the strength of what happened; it was all off center. Edie on one level was an unparalleled exhibitionist, but on another level she was very shy.

I think the thing about Edie, her antic quality had a lot to do with her charm.

She would go to any length to please. She needed to be accepted really on a visceral level, not the way most of us needed to be accepted—kind of casually.

I believe the reason she and I worked together very well was because she liked me and trusted me.

—FRED EBERSTADT

I'LL HAVE TO PUT more

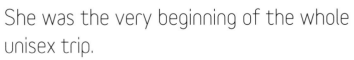

She was the very beginning of the whole unisex trip.

—BETSEY JOHNSON

She would be very apologetic. She would have some cock-and-bull story about something, the elevator jammed or whatever, and you'd have to be in love with her to believe it. But I do think the same reason that Edie and Marilyn Monroe were so chronically late was this anxiety, which if you like, in the end, is what killed them both.

And also, this terrific desire to be liked, to be needed, to be admired, and the thing that also is a tragic mistake there is the confusion of attention with love, and love with attention. There certainly is an overlap, but I don't think they were able to distinguish which was which.

—FRED EBERSTADT

Of course it was very economical, a very cheap, repeatable costume, which to her was tights and a baggy top.

—DANNY FIELDS

**It's all I have to wear.**

**—EDIE**

The leotards and the shirt, I mean, that's what every girl wants. That's all you need in the world. It was like the underground version of the little black dress with the pearls.

—BILLY NAME

She had a little thing for fur. Leopard.

—DANNY FIELDS

She loves "the idea of light hair and dark eyes." She emphasizes them with blue and grey watercolor paint instead of eye shadow.

*NEW YORK TIMES*, 1964

**I really like good, beautiful clothes. I love the space, Courrèges things. I love Rudi Gernreich. I hate to go through seventeen buttons. i'm nervous enough going someplace.**

**EDIE**

**Should I have smiling eyes today?**

**—EDIE**

I never had that much to do with Edie Sedgwick. I've seen where I have had, and read that I have had, but I don't remember Edie that well. I remember she was around, but I know other people who, as far as I know, might have been involved with Edie. Uh, she was a great girl. An exciting girl, very enthusiastic. She was around the Andy Warhol scene, and I drifted in and out of that scene, but then I moved out of the Chelsea hotel. We, me and my wife, lived on the third floor in 1965 or '66, when our first baby was born. We moved out of that hotel maybe a year before *Chelsea Girls*, and when *Chelsea Girls* came out, it was all over for the Chelsea hotel.

**—BOB DYLAN**

In all that time, there was one night that we were alone together in her apartment, and she said, "Danny, I don't really know anything about you. Let's talk about you. This is what I've been wondering, and this is what I've been wondering about myself. Where does this lead, where does this go?" That "You've always been so good to me. You've always been so nice, and I don't know anything about you" became "What do you think I should do?" in a very short time.

**—DANNY FIELDS**

People were telling her that she should concern herself with being a very famous star, putting in her mind that she was the greatest thing since Greta Garbo or Marilyn Monroe—she owed it to herself to be that famous. She didn't know what to do. She began to get qualms. She told me I was her guru at one point, and I said, "I refuse the challenge. I'll be nobody's guru, darling. I can't even guru myself." She really wanted some guidance very badly; she wanted a spiritual moment. And nobody gave it to her.

**—ONDINE**

Edie would still vacillate between enjoying the camp of making movies with us and worrying about her image, and by vacillate I mean she'd go back and forth from hour to hour. She could be standing, talking to a reporter, and she'd look over at us and giggle, then tell him something arch like, "I don't mind being a public fool—as long as I'm communicating myself and reaching people." That was one side of her, putting the media on like that. But fifteen minutes later, she'd be having a dead serious tantrum that she wasn't being taken seriously as an actress. It was a little insane.

—ANDY WARHOL, *POPism*

At that time, she really was being courted by the Grossmans. Her [question] was: Should I stay with this crowd referred to by the Grossman crowd as "those art faggots" or should I align myself with the very powerful emerging Albert Grossman stable, which was the rock 'n' roll hetero-sexual world? I think the Grossmans said to her, "You can be a *real* movie star, you can be a *real*, genuine . . ." They had this thing for genuine, and Andy had this thing for fraudulent. But it really was reversed, because what Andy thought was fraudulent was genuine to us, and what the Grossmans thought was genuine was a little bit fraudulent.

—DANNY FIELDS

She was very tempted, and I gather Bob Dylan was very infatuated with her, as every living male in the history of the world was.

—DANNY FIELDS

She did visit us in the country and I did see her in the city . . . I don't know if she was always with Neuwirth because she was, you know, like, Albert became kind of friends with her as well, right? She had such a great energy . . . She was something of a wild child but there was such an inno-cence about her and a childlike thing at the same time . . . She was just so sweet, you know. There was just no malice in her.

—SALLY GROSSMAN

Charlie Baccis said, "Edie's back in town." "From where?" "From Wood-stock."

—CHUCK WEIN

I backed out of a film I was supposed to do for Andy Warhol. I refused to do it because I got scared. . . . Some insane people from, ah, what was the name of that university, not Columbia but . . . They were quite insane, these people that were backing the film. Anyway, the people broke in to my apartment in the middle of the night and threatened me, and I had a police lock and two other locks, and they broke the door down. Threatened me about the contract and I was, you know, half out of it anyway so he split and left the door splintered behind him. The contract was broken and the star never appeared.

**—EDIE**

[Andy] just realized she was kind of selfish when she said, "Please don't show my films anymore. Mr. Grossman thinks they'd be bad for my reputation now that I'm going to become a film actress." Which he thought was rather peculiar, since nobody was interested in her except once every four months . . . somebody saw the film and then somebody wrote about it for one day, and nobody even saw the films. They saw her picture in the magazines, thanks to Andy.

—PAUL MORRISSEY

Albert [Grossman] was very shrewd, and Albert would want everything for himself. And if Albert was involved, he would've known about the films and he might've told Edie to, you know, not show the films.

—JERRY SCHATZBERG

She was just sort of saying, "Please don't do this. I'm going to go up to Woodstock. Mr. Grossman thinks I should be in a movie. They're planning for Bob to be in the movie, and I'll be in the movie with him."

—PAUL MORRISSEY

It was a strange evening because she was trying to assert herself, and anybody could assert themselves with Andy. It wasn't hard . . . It was just the three of us, and Andy, for some strange reason. had heard that very day, something that she didn't know, and he said, "Edie, do you realize that yesterday or today, Bob Dylan got married?" And she sort of turned white almost. She was really surprised. So I don't know, I guess she hoped for better connections to Dylan going up there. Who knows what she had in her head.

—PAUL MORRISSEY

Everyone knew she was the real heroine of *Blonde on Blonde*.

—PATTI SMITH

I'm a little nervous about saying anything about the artist [Andy], because it kind of sticks him right between the eyes, but he deserves it. He really fucked up a great many young people's lives.

—EDIE

# PHOTOGRAPHING EDIE: JERRY SCHATZBERG

Fashion photographer Jerry Schatzberg photographed Edie early in 1966 at the request of Albert Grossman. After a full night of taking pictures, Edie and Jerry went to the Apollo. ★

I had been photographing Bob Dylan for a little while, and they really liked the photographs that were coming out . . . I think Dylan and Bobby Neuwirth had become friendly with Edie, and they wanted Albert to meet her . . . I think Dylan wanted he and Albert to do something with her because they just felt there was something there. There was a sort of magic in her. Just looking at her was magic. And Albert called me and asked me if I would photograph her. I said yes . . . And I have a funny story with that because I was walking the street before I photographed her, and I ran into Andy and, I think it was Barbara Rubin. She was a documentary filmmaker, I think, yeah, and Andy said, "Ohhhh, what're you doin'?" I said, "Oh well, you know, I'm gonna photograph Edie." We went on talking, split, and when I got back to my studio I got a call from Barbara, who said, "Oh, Andy wants to know if you would do five minutes of footage of Edie for his film?" I said, "Okay." I had a 16mm camera and thought it would be interesting, thought I would play around with it. Ten minutes later she called again and said, "Oh, Andy would like to know if he can come along and do five minutes of you doing five minutes of Edie." I said, "Okay." Then five minutes later she called and said, "Can I come along, also?" I said, "Yeah, you can all come along." Forty people showed up. The whole Velvet Underground, Nico and Lou Reed and just everybody, and they stayed in the studio. We went in the dressing room, and I think I remember Andy was shooting, I guess Barbara was shooting, I was shooting, and I heard [someone] in the background, it was Gerard Malanga, said, "But Andy, there's no film in the camera." He said, "Oh, it doesn't matter."

—JERRY SCHATZBERG

I had met Edie before. Edie used to hang out with Andy a lot, and Andy used to come to my club . . . I was part owner in a discothèque [Ondine's] . . . and I'd see her at different parties and functions . . . The filming happened first, and then I cleared the studio out, so they were gone when I photographed her . . . I'm sure she felt relaxed, and since we knew each other, she, you know, we just had a great time. As a matter of fact, from there we went up to the Apollo, and I don't remember who we saw. Might've been Otis Redding . . . I do remember that I was impressed with how vulnerable she was. There's sort of a trust that, when you go to the doctor, you have to trust the doctor. If you go to a photographer at one point, you have to trust the photographer. Edie just probably, once she commits to it, I don't know if she says yes to everybody that wanted to photograph her, but once she does, she knows what she's doing in terms of committing to it. And I think she trusts what she should.

I don't think she could help but flirt. Just the way she talked to you and looked at you, she was flirting all the time, in her way. I mean, maybe I accept it as flirting, but maybe she just thought that's what life was.

You've seen the photograph that I did where I have different images of her, and that's because I felt that Edie just had all of the different Edies there, and the more I've read about her and the more I know about her, I think it's true.

I like her type of energy because she was, she seemed like she was, always up.

I felt she was quite genuine with me, and I don't think, with somebody like Bobby Neuwirth, that she would do anything but be honest and open, and he evidently loved her. Dylan loved her. I mean everybody loved her because she had that energy.

She didn't have to try. She was just there.

**—JERRY SCHATZBERG**

I know they dated a lot. They went together a lot. They were really compatible, and that's a conservative way of saying they were really in love.

—JERRY SCHATZBERG

When I first went to photograph Dylan, there was this presence there that was very protective, and I'd say to myself this guy's a pain in the ass, but it turns out he was really doing what he was supposed to do. He was there to protect Dylan from the bullshit . . . He was doing a great job, and he was funny, he was clever . . . I didn't know for a long time that he was an artist, that he was a musician, that he was all those things, you know. He wasn't pushing himself in any way. He was just protecting Dylan who was, at that point, needed protection from the public, from different things.

—JERRY SCHATZBERG

She'd been in the Chelsea for a few months when she went home to Santa Barbara for the Christmas of 1966—a magical time for all loonies anyway—to visit her parents. It was an unfortunate idea. They had some queer old New England WASP family idea of, well, it's okay if she spends thirty thousand dollars the first year and forty thousand dollars the second year as long as she gets married the third year and gets herself suitably taken care of for the rest of her life. But when it appeared that she was not going to get herself a nice young polo player, and didn't want to either, it became a question of her parents' not being able to afford to have her independent.

I tried to reach Edie on the phone in California. I pushed and probed, and after a while it turned out she was

sick and couldn't come to the phone; finally I discovered she was in a hospital. "Well, listen, is she in a medical or a psychiatric ward?" It turned out she was in the psychiatric ward. All very confusing. I knew she was not crazy or trying to kill herself.

Edie's father finally came to the telephone. He seemed rather proud when he told me how he had committed her. I guess it was the only way they could think of controlling her . . . hand out the job to a professional. If you can't get your windows clean, hire a window-washer. I told him that I had several lawyers in Los Angeles. If she wasn't at home to answer the phone the next afternoon I was going to get the lawyers, who were poised in Los Angeles to rescue her. He tried to neutralize the situation by saying, "Well, please come out here, and if

FIRST LOVE

you can't afford it, I'll send you an airplane ticket." I remember saying that putting her in a psychiatric ward was so out of keeping with the holiday spirit. Something I said worked: They let her come home.

When I finally reached Edie on the phone, she called out to me: "Get me out of here! I'm a prisoner." Shortly afterwards she was on a plane back to New York, where she arrived smiling and completely covering up the discomfort she had experienced at home. She had a certain puritanical way of not letting her blues get in the way of her lifestyle.

—BOB NEUWIRTH

It took me quite a few immature years of a lot of sex and a lot of pleasure and a lot of nothing, you know? And then I fell in love with someone, and I really learned about sex: making love, loving, giving . . . It just completely blew my mind. It kind of drove me a little insane, too. I was like a sex slave and the minute he'd leave me alone, I felt so empty and so lost, I guess, if I wasn't in the act of lovemaking. I could make love 48 hours, 48 hours, 48 hours one period after another without getting tired. I really enjoyed it. I really loved this man, but it didn't work out . . . The only real true and passionate and lasting love scene ended in, practically in the psychopathic ward.

—EDIE

Man, that was a terrible night. Some little model had called to say she was at the airport and asked where she should go. Edie had taken the message from my answering service and she thought I was not being straight with her. She was in a fury. She burned her cigarette out in my face. It was at some club. I dragged her out into a limousine.

—BOB NEUWIRTH

I really flipped out. Bobby said, let's go to a party. They're having an underground movie and I being the underground Warhol heiress, queen, star, socialite, blah. These underground filmmakers, I can't remember their names, were there making a film, and Bobby really wanted to go and, oh, I had a bad scene with him, in the beginning, I pulled out a knife and I wasn't going to let him out the door until he made love to me. I just get really dreadful. But we went, and I went through the scene. It was filmed, and I really was furious at Bobby. I said, now I'm going to leave this party, I'm fed up. He said, all right, because he met all the people he wanted to meet and . . . so we got out into my limousine and he said, where would you like to eat? And I thought I was going to explode. I screeched at him, why the hell can't you make up your own mind where we're going to eat? Why do I have to make all the decisions? . . . I got madder and madder as we went along, because he didn't say another word. I was so furious that I pressed the button, rolled down the glass plate between the seats, and told the chauffeur that this man was molesting me and that he was a junkie. And then I was so horrified by what I said, so flipped out by that, I jumped out of the car in front of oncoming traffic . . . I got bruised, badly, badly bruised but no broken bones, and I was at a total loss as to what to do. I mean, I was conscious and I wasn't destroyed at all, and I'd done such a terrible thing. The hotel people carried me in and Bobby carried me in, but I had to pretend I was unconscious because I couldn't comprehend the fact that I had tried to get him busted. I'd tried to hurt him seriously. He's the only person I've ever gotten violent about. Of course, I take out whatever violence comes into my system much more heavily on myself than on anyone else, but this was a pretty tight squeeze. If I hadn't jumped out of the car like a maniac, they would have carted him off on my word. I was a celebrity. I was in a much more powerful position than a shady Lower East Side character like Bobby.

**—EDIE**

A guy in New York, somehow connected with the Warhol Factory, I know that they had a relationship. At this point, I couldn't tell you how serious. My best recollection is that it was something that they both maybe wanted to work out and make a strong commitment to. For whatever reasons, it didn't work out. I don't know who left, who fell away first or whatever, but I know that he was a significant other to her for some extended period of time, not just a casual acquaintance.

**—MICHAEL POST**

The brief period of Edie's incandescent openness to life seemed to me to be coming to an end. She had a wonderful appetite for all that life had to offer and for having fun with it that seemed to me to be clouding over, to be dimming, through drugs, though I didn't know what, but she seemed to be a coarser, sadder person. I could see that things were beginning to spiral out of control. And that's when and why Bobby was, I thought, so good for her. Both before and after Bobby, there was no order to her drug-ridden life.

**—DONALD LYONS**

There was a sense of desperation, the way she was obsessed with him and . . . I can't say that he was really capable of containing that kind of, I don't know what to call it, that kind of falling apart, that kind of coming loose, from her. And she tried everything she could to get him to love her. She would buy him things, she would do all kinds of things . . . It was a painful relationship to watch. You can understand it from a psychological point of view . . . The object that isn't available. The blueprint for love was associated with abandonment for her.

**—DOMINIQUE ROBERTSON**

Bob Neuwirth had been working with me on other projects, and he was a very close friend with Edie Sedgwick, who was living in the Chelsea hotel, which is also where I was living. It was a wonderful period. This is about 1967, and Edie was in California, so we got in touch with her. I remember we met her on the plane when it landed in New York, and she came first class with bare feet and sort of pajamas on. She was very heavily into various forms of drugs, and was not averse to drinking. And it was Bob Neuwirth's job to look after her, but she looked right, she looked the part.

**—RICHARD LEACOCK**

I knew Bobby slightly before Edie. I liked the intelligence, the sharpness, the wit of Bobby very much, and around the time that he met Edie and began to escort her to these parties, he struck me as an ordering force in her life.

**—DONALD LYONS**

I remember him saying, "Don't ask me to be a nursemaid. I can't do it. I can't take it."

**—RICHARD LEACOCK**

I thought he was a life raft in the world she was drifting into and very much approved of the relationship and thought he was a good guy. In which opinion I am virtually alone amongst some of the Factory people. He was indeed somebody that she loved very much, and that was very loving of her, and that helped her a great deal.

**—DONALD LYONS**

She certainly was very game to go along with all these crazy things we were doing. The distortion, nothing looked real—we were deliberately trying to get away from reality. She went along with that. The play starts out with the animal trainer of the circus, and the characters of the play are all depicted as animals. So we put Edie into a lion's cage, and she

liked that. She was also very difficult. He had a tough time with her getting it to sort of stick, because she didn't have a great work ethic, if you know what I mean. He was very important in getting it glued there. Also very difficult. She was not easy. If she didn't have the things she craved. He worried a lot about her.

**—RICHARD LEACOCK**

Anyway, we drifted apart. It started off with her mistreating herself. I couldn't believe that a person of such intelligence would mistreat herself to that extent. But I'm sure, reflecting on it, that it was caused by desperation and a lack of outlet for that incredible energy.

**—BOB NEUWIRTH**

He very much disapproved of drugs. The minute he'd leave me I felt so empty and so lost. If I wasn't in the act of love-making, I'd be scheming about how to get drugs.

—EDIE

## CIAO! MANHATTAN
## BLACK AND WHITE SHOOT

# I tried to bake a sweet potato and the oven exploded.

**—EDIE**

She's mischievous. Terribly mischievous. And she enjoys collaborating and colluding in this mischief, which is enchanting. So she'll encourage you to join her in the mischief, and it's cosmic mischief that is masquerading as dysfunction.

**—JOHN PALMER**

***[The exploding potato burned her hands and singed the tip of her nose.] It's not going to interfere with the film. I heal miraculously. I've been in an auto accident and another fire. They thought I'd need plastic surgery, but I haven't a scar . . . No, I don't think I'm accident-prone, but it's strange . . .***

**—EDIE**

I think she wanted to be out of control.

**—L. M. KIT CARSON**

She wasn't here, the way she would move and the way she would comport. And that was one of the reasons people would be sitting around her, astonished that a person could be doing this in real time as a living being.

**—JOHN PALMER**

The first time I recall speaking with her, when we started relating, was, I'm pretty sure, in the Chelsea hotel. I have this strong recollection of me, Chuck, and John going down to the Chelsea to see Edie. Bobby Neuwirth was there, and he was basically playing the role of her lord on-high protector. "What is this about? What's this film about? What are your intentions?" This was, I would say, January or February of '67. It seemed to me that he was in charge and we were asking his permission, almost like his permission for her hand, type-of-thing. I was from a world of applied graphics, working for Preminger on *Hurry Sundown* and all that. Otto Preminger introduced me to Chuck, matter of fact. Chuck was in a world of ethereal manipulations of the art scene, and I'd have switched places with him in a second if I knew what he was doing or what he was trying to do, because he was in a good position. And Neuwirth was in a very distinct world, different from any of that. Bobby Neuwirth sitting there was like Dylan sitting there. I had been in a room with Bob Dylan before, and I knew what that was about at that time, and it was like being in the room with God. Second-coming-of-Christ was the feeling, and Bobby Neuwirth seemed to be St. Peter. So I was very intimidated by him. Given who I was back then, 23, 24 years old but really with the mentality of a 17-year-old. I was very impressionable, so I was terrified by Neuwirth. He was asking questions that I didn't have a clue how to answer, and I was scared shitless something would go wrong and it would be my fault for saying the wrong thing. Chuck launched into his basic low-key, high-powered cosmic rap he did for everyone, but Bobby Neuwirth didn't seem to pay much attention to a thing he said.

**—DAVID WEISMAN**

The first time I saw her I was sitting in my office at Centaur, which was this little, sort of, island of hippie types in the sea of rabbinical jewelry makers. I think it was David and John walked in the door, and Chuck Wein, walked in the door with her, and they sort of were like holding her up. She was very fancily dressed—"this is the leading lady of our movie,"—and you know, look official, so I looked official. I think the meeting lasted about ten minutes. I was kind of taken with her. I saw her frailty, but, uh, her kind of wispiness quality that I liked, and, of course, she was being hyped extensively by the trio. I think Gino Piserchio was there, too, if I remember, but I'm not entirely sure. It was all very, very smart and very chic. In a way, it was sort of like a bunch of grifters. They sort of came in and gave me a big sales thing on it. It was sort of like running away with the circus on one side when she came in. On the other side it was like a very, very slow-motion car crash.

—BOB MARGOULEFF

I have no recollection of interaction between Chuck and Edie. Chuck stuck me with Edie. He said, "Okay Weisman, now she's yours. Your charge, she's your responsibility. And don't lose her because she's tricky." She's elusive, I think that was the word he used . . . It was like, everything was depending on her being around and so forth, and being available, and now I was in charge of her whereabouts. It's the day of the Central Park "be-in" and Chuck and Genevieve are busy conceptualizing the movie with, you know, their amphetamine pokes and their astrological charts, so it's up to me to take care of Edie. In other words, instead of the director taking charge and walking Edie among the thirty thousand flower-children in the sheep meadow that day, making sure the camera follows her doing whatever it is he thought she should be doing, Chuck first needed to, you know, chart the vibes of the universe, and Edie had to be around until he figured it all out. "Just don't lose her." So he stuck her with me, and I lost her in ten minutes. Never had my eyes off her once, but I lost her in ten minutes flat. Don't ask me how. Palmer spotted her, shot that footage of her up on a rock helping some hippies raise a wooden cross, but I never saw her again for the rest of the day.

—DAVID WEISMAN

When they were doing *Ciao! Manhattan*, they had all found Dr. Jake and Dr. Bishop and everybody was shooting up with Bishop's vitamin shots. I guess they had something in them. I don't really know because I didn't do it, and I was afraid to do it.

**—JANE HOLZER**

When people came back from Dr. Roberts' office they looked very healthy, very happy, very energized, very into thousands of ideas that all sort of didn't really go anywhere. I finally got to a place where I would see people coming into my office. This guy Billy, who became a friend of Gino's and me, he was crawling around on the floor, trying to get the cocaine crystals or the speed crystals, or whatever he was looking for, out of the fluff in the carpet.

**—BOB MARGOULEFF**

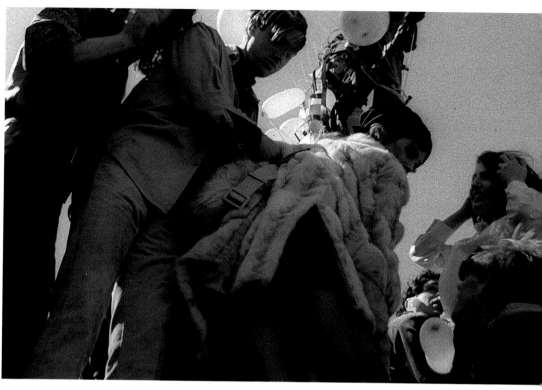

I heard about this doctor who gave vitamin shots, and they were very stimulating and kept you going for quite a while. I was under treatment with vitamin therapy, just multivitamin shots. But I heard about this super deal that this other doctor had. A guy I was going out with at the time told me not to go to him, never to have his shots. So I immediately took them, thinking there must be something special about them . . . And there was. And I went, and that was the beginning of injecting drugs. I went to a doctor for it. I didn't handle it myself until a year later. I turned into a total speed freak for a few months. That's about as long as I could survive, and then I placed myself in the hospital.

**—EDIE**

At that point in time, she was, a lot of those people were, heavy into Methedrine. Alternating between B-12 shots and Methedrine. So we delivered the envelope and promptly watch her, you know, rig up an outfit, you know, pull her bikini down and jab her ass and shoot herself, you know, with some crank, some Methedrine . . . We're a couple of surfers from California, so our eyes are like saucers with this kind of stuff.

**—SEPP DONAHOWER**

The world of the black-and-white footage of *Ciao! Manhattan* was a media pigsty of astrological charts, astral-projection notes and diagrams, pentagrams, flotsam and jetsam from a bunch of different half-baked, hippie-dippie, Eastern, Buddhist, North African, tangerine dream fantasies . . . It was a media pigsty. You never entered a room when there weren't pillows on the floor and everything, the floor covered with this ephemera.

**—DAVID WEISMAN**

But we were kind of play-acting that as well. We have these young people in New York, at the time, making this movie, and we're being DP and star, which for us is a hoot. It's not really real; it is real because we're doing it, and yet we're both just sort of having a ball playing this dance.

**—JOHN PALMER**

I don't know what was in her mind as a plan for the future, because it seemed to be pretty intense in the moment. I don't think she thought about the future.

**—L. M. KIT CARSON**

Even though she was like into some throes of some pretty crazy-ass addiction, you know, and behavior and kind of going down a bad path . . . she'd walk in a room and the conversation would stop even if you weren't looking at her. You know, she sort of had that kind of charisma.

**—SEPP DONAHOWER**

It was a given that she was the classiest of all, most beautiful, the most glamorous, and you moved around her in that way. This was part of her persona.

**—DAVID WEISMAN**

These things are all in simple moments. The way she would jump off the bed when she was happy . . . there's just childlike, okay, there you go, spunky child. That's probably a big hook on why people got her. And she retained that.

**—L. M. KIT CARSON**

She would summarize everything that was going on and blurt out a couple statements that were infinite wisdom at times. She was a very bright and perceptive person. She was always famous for finishing people's sentences. Knew what they were going to say before they said it.

**—SEPP DONAHOWER**

She had this sense of humor about herself and her situation, about the insane capers we were living through. I'd test the boundaries of her sense of play, to see how far she felt comfortable going, always trying to find where she would draw the line and she never drew a line anywhere. There was no line to be drawn. She saw her life as an open book, and she could laugh at every page.

**—DAVID WEISMAN**

Allen Ginsberg was doing... There was some "om" kind of thing. She was, I think, next to me, or maybe we were sitting in a circle in the grass and holding hands and whatever, and she started crying and I mean, she cried with such... It was so emotional that at the time I did not really know.

Now I think maybe drugs had something to do with it, but at the time I was, like, very touched because it seemed extremely sincere... Oh, it was for *Ciao! Manhattan*.

**—LARISSA**

The Margouleffs, Bob's parents, Gene and Ruth, grew more and more astonished and aghast at what was going on. At first they were serving everyone canapés and refreshments, dubious but hoping for the best, because there was a lot of wine around, cheap wine, and later when they left, lots of speed. I remember rumor had it that when they cleaned the pool at Al Roon's the next day, the drains were all clogged with syringes. There was a rumor about a dog; I think Sandy the sound man's dog had eaten all the film. *Ciao! Manhattan* began as this chic thing, and then after the Al Roon's health spa scene, Viva got attention for herself by spreading the rumor that a dog ate the film. See, people don't understand, what part of the film did the dog eat? Was it the work print? The negative? How much did he consume? Was it five frames or five reels, or whatever. The

truth is, no dog ate anything, but that was the ongoing rumor. I think she said it in some article. What ever happened to *Ciao! Manhattan*? Oh, the dog ate the film. I lived in constant shame from early '68 straight through 'til I left for California in the spring of '70. Everyone began asking, "Well, when's the movie gonna be finished?" Or, "Where is it, when can we see it?" I used to go to Max's every night and as I'd walk in the door Mickey, the owner, would say to me, night after night, "Hi David—is it finished yet?" I wouldn't even answer.

**—DAVID WEISMAN**

**The whole place turned into a gigantic orgy, every kind of sex freak, from homosexuals to nymphomaniacs, especially the needle and mainlining scene, losing syringes down the pool drains and blocking up the water infiltration system with broken syringes. Oh, it was really some night... Drinking, guzzling tequila, vodka, and scotch, and bourbon, and shooting up every other half-second, and just going into an incredible sexual tailspin. Gobble gobble gobble gobble. Couldn't get enough of it. It was one of the wildest scenes I've ever been in or ever hope to be in, and I should be ashamed of myself. I'm not, but I should be.**

**—EDIE**

She lived in a brownstone underneath, or above, I can't remember which, Jeff Gates, who was an old friend. She lit herself on fire there. She was smoking, and she was always dropping cigarettes around.

**—GEORGE PLIMPTON**

Burning up money, burning up cigarettes, burning up your mind, burning up traces, your footsteps. Burning up the place she lives in, the Chelsea hotel. You know, burning up.

**—ULTRA VIOLET**

# THE FIRES

## I have an accident about every two years, and one day it won't be an accident.

**—EDIE**

I've never seen her more beautiful. She puts on a pair of red leotards and red, tight cotton top. I weed out the seeds and twigs from the pot and fill one-eighth full Camel with the Acapulco Gold. We get exceedingly high. She tells me how she wanted to run away from the mad publicity for an entire year, how it all frightened her, how transparent it all was, and how the men are so desperate for the faceless publicity—stark-raving mad seeking acquisitions they want so desperately. How sorry Edie feels for them. How composed she remains . . . I leave Edie falling asleep in her apartment.

**—GERARD MALANGA, IN HIS DIARY, ON SEEING EDIE THE NIGHT OF HER APARTMENT FIRE IN 1966**

She was so beautiful, limp in the shirt, the striped shirt, maybe bare-legged, no, the tights. I see her holding a cigarette in the fireman's arms, and you can just imagine the look on that fireman's face because he's walking down the ladder this way. You can't walk down a ladder that way. He stopped and posed with her for that picture. Can you walk down a ladder this way? I don't think so. Tell us. Oh, firemen in the audience, write to us. Tell us, when you carry a movie star down the stairs, down a ladder, how do you do it?

**—RENE RICARD**

I went to the hospital to see her, and I remember her being shaken up, but not terrified. I think it was Lenox Hill Hospital. I stayed with her an hour or so, half an hour, and she was just like a frightened kid, a frightened child.

**—JUDY FEIFFER**

When I brought Leonard Cohen in to meet her at the Chelsea, she had been shopping or shoplifting, with her you never knew . . . She bought candles and arranged them on the non-working mantel. She and Brigid were in some kind of, "Let's paste sequins upon a *mah na mah* until it's covered in sequins" and whatever. Part of their afternoon activities. Leonard said, "This woman is in great danger." And I said, "Why do you say that?" And he said, "That particular arrangement of candles." Some African or voodoo or whatever, I don't know, it could just be Leonard and his genius. He knew a woman before he met her, any woman. He said, "This is very unlucky. She should change this around." And she just laughed it off as, "Jesus I've heard some stupid superstitions in my time." And sure enough, it wasn't long before the room burned, and she managed to just get out by crawling along the floor in the burning room and reaching for the metal doorknob.

**—DANNY FIELDS**

I remember Genevieve Charbin phoning and waking me up. We were all living on 43rd Street in my Tudor City duplex, me, Genevieve, Chuck, Paul. Edie was living at the Chelsea. And Genevieve woke me in the middle of the night and said, "There's a fire at the Chelsea, you gotta get down there right away." I don't know how I got Margouleff's Porsche, but I got a hold of his red Porsche speedster, and he never got it back again, but I went down and rescued Edie. She was on the floor of the lobby. I remember firemen, and long hoses snaked on the floor. I remember Edie all covered with soot and curled up on the marble lobby floor, shivering, naked under blankets.

—DAVID WEISMAN

She lost her cat in that fire, too, and it was a cat that Bob Dylan had given her.

—DANNY FIELDS

I didn't know anything about it. Somebody said, "Oh, she set fire to the hotel," you know, come on. I was the first Chelsea girl who lived at the Chelsea. I saw so many fires here. I was there the night Jim Morrison set fire to that redhead's hair with a bottle of cognac.

—RENE RICARD

Edie was living the high scene, the movie starlet scene over on the tab, over at the Chelsea hotel, with a closet of my father's very expensive fur coats in the closet, and suddenly I get this phone call: "Man, you've gotta get over to the Chelsea hotel. There's been a fire at the Chelsea, and Edie was burned, and her room burned down and ..." I get over there and there's all the fur coats toasted in the closet, the smell of smoke rafting out of the windows, fire truck downstairs. And there's Edie standing there like, you know, with soot on her face and a little mini-dress and stuff, swaddled in gauze on both hands. Right. What to do, what to do, right?

—BOB MARGOULEFF

The perilous descent to safety.

12C      DAILY NEWS, WEDNESDAY, OCTOBER 19, 1966

Peter Hoppner crawls off top-floor ledge onto ladder where Fireman Joseph McDonald waits to lend a helping hand. See the foto at left.

## Seven Families Saved From East Side Blaze

Firemen, responding quickly to blaze in an apartment at 16 E. 63d St. early yesterday, rapidly contained the fire. Before they were through they had evacuated seven families, mostly in their nightclothes (foto left) and an actress. The fire, of unknown cause, broke out in the 3½-room quarters of actress Edith Sedgewych, 24, and engulfed her apartment. Miss Sedgewych, suffering smoke poisoning, was taken to Hospital.

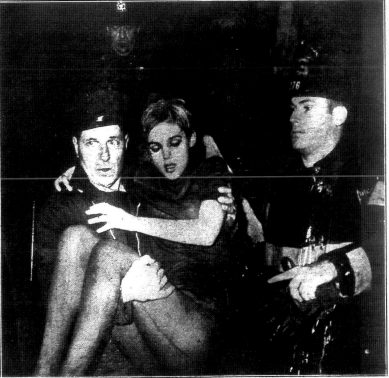

(NEWS fotos by Jim Hughes)

Fire Chief George Gekrish carries Edith Sedgewych from flaming building. She suffered smoke poisoning.

We started this affair out of me creating a character for her to play. That made her interested. I was in love with the character, and she was the character, period. So it was astounding to me that we actually began to do this in three-dimensional reality.

She was smart, she was sensual. She was a real full-time experience.

We moved from hotel to hotel, because she at the time had become notorious for burning her rooms in the Chelsea. And we ended up in the Warwick hotel, and we signed in as being married, because this is how we can get into a hotel. Otherwise they won't let us come in.

Then I began to notice that her behavior was unsequential. It became erratic, and I couldn't know what was going on.

# THE WARWICK

So it'd come and go. And then one late afternoon I came back and I was shaving because we were going out and I saw on the floor a little plastic sleeve, and I picked it up and I realized it was the sleeve at the end of a hypodermic needle, and I bring it out and I go, like, "Okay, what's going on?" She showed me that she had drugs and that she was injecting, and I put them all away. I called up the Factory and Andy said, "I can't come, but I'll send some people." So some people came, and they laid out all the drugs on the bed, and they went, like, "Oh mm-ah, this is, mm-oh, wow, where did you get this?" And they took it all away. And then I had to stay, taking care of her while she came down, and that was like a day. And then it was, like, two days, and then it was, like, wait a minute, she's getting drugs again somehow, and it was, like, three days. And I hadn't slept, and I didn't know what to do. But you have to understand, this comes at the end of a very full affair. There was a lot of romance in it. There was a lot of love in it. But I was losing control of a situation, and I couldn't read the situation, didn't know how to make it different. So I called her doctor; this relationship started when I took her out of the hospital. And he said, "Leave." I said, "I can't leave."

—L. M. KIT CARSON

She felt as far as her father was concerned, she could have been dead. That he didn't care.

—L. M. KIT CARSON

I guess I should call this the Siege of the Warwick . . . but left alone with a substantial supply of speed I forgot that I was heavily addicted to barbiturates, and I started having strange convulsive behavior. This was after I was done, well, I was shooting up every half hour, every twenty minutes on the half hour, thinking with each fresh shot I'd knock this nonsense out of my system, this physical disability I began to notice, namely convulsions, which lasted eight hours, during which I entertained myself while hanging on to, head down, hanging on to the bathroom sink, with my hind feet stomped against the drawer, trying to hold myself steady enough so I wouldn't crack my stupid skull open. I entertained myself by doing a tape and making up five female voices, all different personalities. A really fabulous tape. I can't remember the details of it now, and it was lost in one of my fires, but it was quite brilliant, I think. At the end of it, when I realized that I had to get barbiturates in order to stop the convulsions, I, something was zingy in my head, I just kept thinking if I pop enough speed, I'll knock the daylights out of my system and then none of this nonsense will go on. None of this flailing around the room and sweating like a pig and, woof, it was a heavy scene, and when I finally cooled down to an extent where I thought I was calm and cool and collected, far be it from the reality, but comparatively, I was in pretty good shape.

So I flipped on a little muumuu, ran down barefoot, taking the stairs to the lobby, and my eye caught a mailman's jacket and then a sack of mail in the hallway, and before I knew what I was doing, I whipped on the jacket, flipped the bag over my shoulder, and flew out the door, whistling a happy tune, got halfway around the block, and suddenly I thought, my God, this is a federal offense, fooling around with the mail. So I turned around and rushed back and, bam, the manager was there and he just . . . ordered me in the back office, standing there. And so I began to articulate it as cautiously as I could, and inquire as to what I might be able to be held for. Not one of them would answer me. They telephoned an ambulance from Bellevue, packed me into it, five policemen. I wasn't much of a match against them, and was rushed to Bellevue, which is one of the most insane institutions I have ever walked the hallways of. I proceeded to tell the doctors, while I was back in convulsions again, which was really a drag, and I proceeded to tell all the attending doctors and nurses and students that I was heavily addicted to speed and barbiturates, that I'd run out of barbiturates, and that I'd over-shot speed, so that I was in this state of convulsion. I could speak sanely, but I behaved . . . All my motor nerves were going wild, crazy, flipped out, insane motions, so I looked like I was out of my mind. If you just listened to what I had to say, it was sane, but if you looked at me, you wouldn't bother to listen, and none of them did. Oh, God, it was a nightmare. Finally, about six big attendants came and then held me down and put me on a stretcher and I . . . They just terrified me, just their force against me, and I got twice as bad. I just flipped, and I told them if they'd just let go of me I could calm down, I could stop kicking and fighting and being so terrified, but they wouldn't listen. And then they started this nightmare, telling each other what I was going through, what stages of hallucinations of, you know, hallucinations I was in, how I imagined myself an animal of a sort. All these things, totally unreal to my mind, and just guesses on their part . . . oh, it was insane. And then they plunged a great big needle into my butt and, bam, out I went for two whole days, unconscious . . .

It was one of the most terrifying experiences I've ever been through.

—EDIE

And about three days later, the police show up at my house in Paris, Texas, and say, "Your wife is in Bellevue." "Oh, yeah, yes. My wife is in Bellevue."

—L. M. KIT CARSON

Mind you, I had a life, I had a career—we all did—and so didn't have time to be with her at all times . . . She stayed on the high plane; the rest of us ascended there. Life on the high plane left her finally abandoned.

**–DONALD LYONS**

FALLING

I feel guilty. One didn't know what to do with this incredible charm and life force and willingness to live and cleverness at seizing what is beautiful in life. One didn't want to say . . . Because, after all, she was evolving into something that had not been seen yet, the international superstar, whatever we should call it. She was becoming the Edie Sedgwick of the day; there had been nothing like it.

—DONALD LYONS

There's drug use like the way we saw on Fishers Island, when it was rather beautiful and exciting. This was a couple years later, but it seemed like an eon later . . . people looked damaged by what was going on. She didn't look good anymore. Her hair was bleached white. She looked tragic: Her eyes were dark, black makeup. One of the things she was doing while the camera was grinding away on her was putting on makeup. I remember getting bored. I was like, "I know, it's supposed to be really, really cool and exciting, but . . ."

—ROBIN SEDGWICK

I mean, some of the things, like, really went way astray. I should have, maybe, responded more, but somehow I didn't. Now I look back, I wonder about listening to the sound of my own wheels, what motivated me during that time, what made me be a party to it.

—BOB MARGOULEFF

I think as she got older, the recklessness got stronger, and it really would have been far more brave for her to try to do otherwise than what she was doing. But she gave in to it. She was the opposite of brave. She let the tide carry her along. And the tide was a destructive one, and she became a smaller and smaller speck as she simply let herself be swept along in its flow.

—ROBIN SEDGWICK

She leads you sort of on a Dante-esque tour of the lower depths.

—GEORGE PLIMPTON

She came up to me [in Gracie Square] like a little orphan. Like a beautiful little girl in this hospital gown and just looking bruised in every way and trembling and just said hello with those big eyes. It was like her sadness or her misery transcended any setting or any drug or anything. She didn't look like she had a place to go back to or a place to have another chance.

—LIBBY TITUS

I think her tragedy in one sense was simply that her immense abilities, her immense enthusiasm, her immense appetites had nothing to devour, and therefore became turned on themselves as it were. In retrospect, she should have entered school. She should have done something real. She should have designed clothes, something. But she was Edie. There was nothing that Edie was except EDIE.

—DONALD LYONS

There wasn't anything like that for her out there. There wasn't somewhere to go. There wasn't someone to be. There was just the moment, and that need to try to bring it all inside of her, to fill the void.

—ROBIN SEDGWICK

She was sliding deeper down the cliff of her own manufacture.

—DANNY FIELDS

We were naughties. We wanted to be naughties, and we were naughties.

—ULTRA VIOLET

By the end of the sixties, the rate of attrition was really showing up. A lot of people didn't make it. It was a great party, but not everybody made it to morning.

—BIBBE HANSEN

There were so many people OD'ing at the Chelsea or dying in a fire or jumping off the roof that it was like an endless stream of loss, and so they all blend into one feeling of, "What's going on? Why are all those people ending like that?" Drugs were a big part. They were basically the biggest part of it. I remember Andrea Whips, and she was every night at the round table at the back of Max's, and I remember her once saying to me, "You are so lucky you never were in an Andy movie." Well, I was never in an Andy movie because I was too shy to appear in front of a camera. But she said it in a strange way, and a few days later she jumped off a balcony of her mother's apartment on Park Avenue. So it was a mixture of, you know, exposing yourself and taking drugs and wanting to be loved by Andy, be the only one, you know, or by Jimi Hendrix, like this young woman who overdosed at the Chelsea. I was told to take care of her, but, you know, who can take care of people who are in that situation?

—LARISSA

I remember my father telling me, "Edie can't help being fucked up. Bad things happened to Edie."

—BIBBE HANSEN

The first thing you saw when you walked into Max's Kansas City was a Chamberlain car wreck, you know, squashed, and then standing next to it, Edie Sedgwick sort of rotating on an invisible pedestal. Two symbols of destruction.

—DANNY FIELDS

The one thing that was intriguing about Edie was not just the fact that she was attractive and sexy and all that, and a little on the wild side, but she really, her intellect, I think, is one of the things that really hooked people, because this gal was no dummy, and even in a whack-job state, she could make some very, could say some very profound things. She would see what's going on in a room or make a statement about what was happening then, it was so, you know, that would summarize it, and make it all so clear and relevant.

—SEPP DONAHOWER

She was intriguing, entertaining, and she had a broken heart, which could draw me in.

—DOMINIQUE ROBERTSON

She had such a gift for expression for being alive. Who knows what she would have been able to do? It was a doubtful future.

—DONALD LYONS

At that time she was like on Mars.

—SEPP DONAHOWER

# chapter three: CALIFORNIA

When Edie drove back into California, two college-age surfers taking turns at the wheel, she was arriving in a strange land. She stayed briefly with Sepp, then found her way back closer to the action at the Castle, at the time Nico and Jim Morrison were there, and had a fling with Dino Valenti—famous for writing "Get Together." From there, she returned briefly to New York before landing in Isla Vista, a suburb of Santa Barbara, where she underwent a course of shock treatments. California's sixties culture was a whole new thing: Hippies looking to slow down rather than speed up. Though a nature girl at heart, Edie wasn't easily taken in by all the smiles and flowers. She took off her shoes—and sometimes her clothes—like always. Despite the constraints of her new existence, she swept through the social strata. She found audiences for her stories among bikers, college students, and fellow patients. ★

The *Ciao!* filmmakers were now spread across the globe. After Chuck had departed from the project, Weisman and Margouleff were left with a hundred hours of Palmer's 35mm black and white cinematography, in the shambles of a work-print that was cut into bits by speeding editors.. David Weisman and John Palmer had kept in touch with Edie throughout her hospital stays in New York, but it was Henry Geldzahler who alerted the filmmakers to the fact that Edie, whom he had visited briefly in Santa Barbara, was more beautiful than ever. David came out to California to meet with Edie, and in early 1970, Weisman believed he might have found financing to complete *Ciao! Manhattan*. John Palmer and his fiancée Janet Brooke arrived from London and were employed by Edie's mother to look after her. They all lived together in Santa Barbara near Cottage Hospital, where Edie had been born. Edie was now back close to home, but not at home. She couldn't return to the ranch to ride the horses she loved as a child, in part because her doctor felt it was best to keep her apart from her mother. By this point she was seeing a prominent local psychiatrist daily while immersed in the planning of the *Ciao!* color shoot. Two teenagers, Jeff Briggs and Wesley Hayes, were hijacked into being both actors and grips for the film, which became a bit of a traveling circus. John Palmer and David Weisman began recording tapes with Edie, using her stories to guide their new vision. Meanwhile they gathered their forces in preparation for the shoot, which this time would be in color and would serve as a device to frame what had already been filmed in black-and-white three years earlier in New York. By mid-1970, everyone converged in Los Angeles. Bob Margouleff, his family's financial backing of the film long since over, came back not as producer but as soundman. Kjell Rostad, an actor in the New York footage who would be the gaffer and co-cameraman with Palmer on the new shoot, and Eduardo Lopez de Romaña, who would work on the film's electronics engineering and post-production aspects, drove non-stop from New York to the Santa Monica Pier, afraid to turn off their engine for fear the car would die forever. ★

Edie would dance all afternoon to James Taylor's *Sweet Baby James* during the time leading up to the *Ciao!* pool shoot. There is no way to know which lyrics spoke to her most, but in the title song Taylor evokes Stockbridge, Massachusetts, her family's ancestral haunt, and Boston. Edie herself had been a "moonlight lady," and Bob Neuwirth had called her Lady. Her character in *Ciao!*, a part clearly based on her, was named Susan, just like the heroine of "Fire and Rain." Taylor's album mythologizes the West the same way Edie's father's art had. Or it may have just been the gentle and soothing nostalgia of James' voice that seemed right to her. Maybe she just liked it because he looked so cute on the cover of the album. She had met Mick Jagger, even joked about marrying him, knew Dylan well, hadn't yet met James. Maybe he seemed like promise. Maybe he reminded her of Bob Neuwirth. ★

Sometimes Edie wanted to get back to New York. She wanted to get back to her friends. At other times, she just wanted to run off. Those who cared for her and lived with her say she would just go: Walk through screen doors into the night air and hitchhike away before anyone could stop her. The color footage of *Ciao! Manhattan* was filmed in December 1970 and January 1971. ★

Edie, who had never cooked, made pork chops for Jeff Briggs, as though trying on a domestic role for size. On the day of John and Janet Palmer's wedding, Edie stood at the top of the courthouse steps and asked "Am I getting married?" She played make-believe at Janet and John's wedding and then followed suit with a wedding of her own. Michael Post, a young man who Edie had met in Cottage Hospital when she had just gotten back to California, and who she had seen on and off since then, proposed to her. It was June. Two weeks later, she said, "If we're going to do this, I want to do it now. I don't want to wait any longer." They were married July 24, 1971, on her family's Rancho La Laguna, and by all accounts, Edie was radiant. Though she had fought her whole life to escape the mold of marriage, she began to talk about having children. Four months later, at age 28, she died, suffocating in her sleep, facedown in her pillow. She thought she might be pregnant on the night she died. But that same night she told Michael Post she would leave him soon. She had not let go of her idea of returning to it all in triumph and with bells on. She was restless. Edie wanted a second chance at fame. ★

The day she died, Edie had been at a fashion show being filmed as part of the first reality television series, *An American Family*, for PBS. One of her closest friends from Cambridge and New York, Tommy Goodwin was there as a crew member. How strange to see someone who had been her friend and even her chauffeur during more carefree times. People remember her being drawn to the cameras that night and of her speaking about traveling back to New York. At a party that evening a woman lashed out at Edie, calling her a junkie, among other things. Rather than walk away from the insults, Edie insisted on staying to dissuade the woman of her opinion, saying again and again to Michael that she had to "make her see." Edie was firm in the resolve to tell her life story, and to tell it properly. There is no director credit given on *Ciao! Manhattan*. Everyone who worked on the final part of that film with her talks about her resolve in completing it. Edie directed herself. She died waiting to see if the film would open the doors that had shut and more. ★

At the end of her life Edie became a storyteller. She was reliving her past, injecting her old adventures with humor, introspection, but creating no new ones. Her whole worldview, her self-ascribed purpose, had been yanked out from under her. Perhaps her mind had been so tried by drugs and shock treatment that she could no longer remember the point of her fame, and just craved the sensation of being the center of attention—or maybe she wanted one more chance to tell her story on a larger stage. ★

She was a hottie. I'll admit it. Wolford and I, she sort of took a liking to us because, I think, she was looking for some real friends about that time. Things were tumultuous in her life, I think, at that time . . . thin ice everywhere. It was towards the end of the summer [1967], before school. So it was like we had to get back to California to start class again. I told her that I thought it might be a good idea for her to get out of Dodge, basically, get out of Dodge, or die. She said okay and hopped in the car and boom! We took off to California in my Volkswagen.

It took like fifty-two hours or something, just straight through—zoom—either acid or black beauties. So we got back here [to Los Angeles], and I had this old converted restaurant I lived in called the Hideaway Café, almost really on the campus of USC. The place was all kind of tricked out, and Edie stayed there, I think, about maybe a month. Kind of got her health back 'cause we weren't into shooting speed and stuff. We'd get stoned, but we were more into, you know, smoking a lot of pot, psychedelics, mescaline, California drugs. So she sort of weaned herself . . . she was actually not taking anything. She got real sober. Real straight and healthy and was thinking real clear. She was one of the brighter people I ever met. Anyway, then we got a call one day, some friends of hers had blown into town. Nico and some other people, and they were staying up at this infamous Castle, up in the hills of Los Feliz. Okay, so we trip up to the Castle, and there's a scene going on there. Usually stars, celebrities, musicians, actors, whoever was in town would stay at the Castle 'cause you were guaranteed a good time. Bob Dylan stayed there, Andy stayed there . . .

So anyway, she fell back, kind of, with the New York crowd, and a lot of drugs, and so the New York drugs started up again . . . And then she said she wanted to go stay up there. So went up and got her crap, and I left her there and that was the last I ever saw of her. We were, you know, I think she probably got bored with us 'cause we were a bunch of college guys, and all of a sudden I've got to go to class again.

—SEPP DONAHOWER

It was the legendary weekend. Or weekday or whatever. Edie and Nico were living at the Castle alone and needed me and David Neuman to protect them. From what? I think the house across the street had belonged to Bela Lugosi, so there must have been bats or something . . . And Paul Morrissey said, "WOULD YOU GO UP AND PROTECT THEM!!?" . . . We drove up to the Castle. Edie had left Sepp and was with Dino Valenti then. He wrote this one song: "Come on children, let's all get together, smile on your brother." It became a classic, but it was a one-shotter. Edie was with him up at the Castle . . . [At one point] I went to get my drug stash, and it was completely decimated. I don't know how she did it, but she had, under the eyes and ears and nose of all of us, discovered this secret hiding place . . . Edie had found it and had almost everything. I mean, she left like one of each. When I'd be going through my father's wallet, I would just take TWO of each. I'd take two twenties, three fives, leave like a big wad of each, but she left me one of each. Which of course I had to share with Jim Morrison.

—DANNY FIELDS

**THE TRIP**

**EDIE:** It's all that each individual of his own free will or power has arrived at that state of mind. And it's sort of like a mockery in a way of reality because they think everything is smiles and sweetness and flowers when there is something bitter to taste. And to pretend there isn't is foolish. I mean the ones that wander around and know, at the same time, and yet wear flowers, and they deserve to know flowers. And they've earned the smile.

**PAUL AMERICA:** Well, if they know, then they don't wear flowers.

**EDIE:** There's a difference. You can tell by people's eyes.

*CIAO! MANHATTAN* **TAPES**

Everybody in the sixties was James Dean-ism, or rebelling, so there was a degree of fashion that was associated with that . . . she's doing the same thing everybody else is doing. So Edie comes shooting out of this as an archetype, a paradigm that represents all of what's going on that way. She's perfectly positioned to be this rebellious character, because the wheels are coming off everywhere.

**—JOHN PALMER**

The sixties, you know . . . We started out dancing through the daisies and running over the green hills and you looked over your shoulder and there was a couple bodies dropping, pretty soon you were running for your life through broken glass and there were scary people chasing you.

**—JEFF BRIGGS**

She'd dress up in her soul as a hippie, to be able to experience that, as if it were a fashion. But it's not essentially who she is. There's something deeper that she's working on.

**—JOHN PALMER**

I moved out to Santa Barbara to straighten out, supposedly, and I started using drugs, which I found were plentiful in Isla Vista, around the college campus—UCSB. And then I started rollicking around with all kinds of kids a lot younger than me. Anywhere from 15 to their 20s, but I was kind of in my late 20s. And, uh . . . I had fun, but I really didn't have anyone I particularly loved. And I still don't, except for loving friends.

—EDIE

ISLA VISTA

It wasn't because she wanted to come get into bed with us because the attention was off her. It wasn't a sex thing. It was more that she was the child, and the mummy and daddy were there . . . I think her instinct was like a puppy's or a cat's: "I'm going to push myself into the newspaper when you're reading it."

**—JANET PALMER**

She compressed an awful lot of life into a short period of time, so by the time we get to the end she's used up a lot.

**—JOHN PALMER**

She was a chameleon, you know, that's the first impression. She was very good at the first-impression thing, but then she was different things to different people.

**—JANET PALMER**

I melted on the smile, and then once I was able to get eye contact with her, then I knew I was going somewhere. Her eyes just, they opened up. I mean, they opened up to me.

**—MICHAEL POST**

That was her charm, you see. That whenever she talked to you she could just, she put like an energy on you. She had this ability to make you feel like she's showing herself or only concentrating on you, that you're the only thing that—she's very interested in you. She just made you feel warm. So, there's nothing you can do about it except respond. You never could go away from her. You didn't want to leave first.

**—WESLEY HAYES**

Some people search hard, you know. They search. You can search with nature, you can search with your mind, you can search with your body, you can search with chemicals, you can search, and that's what we're talking about. Is that, the dynamo, the engine that makes things move? Some people search and they search tough, they search hard, they search with their body. There's hunger. There's anger. There's angst. There's thirst. And a person like Edie, I suppose, is given every benefit of that whole generation . . . of that whole nation in conquest and in victory . . . and yet there has to come an apogee; you get as high as you can and you can't get any higher . . . and you're on the cusp of consciousness.

**—EDUARDO LOPEZ DE ROMAÑA**

The car I drove back then was this 1955 Mercedes Benz 300SL. They called it a Gullwing. It was like the ultimate dream car of its era and Edie and I would drive back to the house and we'd get into this whole routine. Inevitably, she would say, "David, could we have the doors open?" And I'd say, "Edie, you know what's gonna happen." "Oh, but it's so fun, and I love the wind." I'd succumb, then we'd zip along the freeway with our doors open like wings, until the cops pulled us over. They'd search her, search me, search the car. She'd be giggling. They'd ask, "what's so funny?" and I'd say, "Nothing is funny, officer." Edie'd giggle like crazy when I was doing this. It was dangerous, it was escapist, it was pushing the limits in a very freakish way. When you drove the Gullwing with the doors open, you had this sensation, especially above sixty, sixty-five miles an hour, at what point are we gonna take off?

—DAVID WEISMAN

She seemed to have an air of confidence about herself being able to mesmerize people. To draw them. There was something about her that, if she walked into this room right now, you'd just say, "Okay. You've got the floor, young lady. Let's hear it. What is it?"

**—MICHAEL POST**

She's telling a story. She understood people, how they were, who they were, who was good or bad or what their motives were. That was a quality about her . . . You could tell that she was more aware of things going on than you were. Like she knew more. She understood people.

**—WESLEY HAYES**

I don't think Edie had too many secrets. She had forgotten what her secrets were.

**—JANET PALMER**

She would talk about what she expected from *Ciao! Manhattan*, what she kind of wanted. She felt like she had this story to get out. She wanted to talk about herself, her experiences. To her, it was a documentary . . . She felt like this was going to be her story . . . Everything that ever happened to her. She seemed to remember everything.

So she was all too willing to want to put that out there. She really thought *Ciao! Manhattan* was gonna be, and I think everyone was kind of hoping that as well, that it was the real story.

**—WESLEY HAYES**

She was totally aware of the fact at all times that she was playing a character that me and John were extrapolating from her real life, and that it was a hoot. It was a hoot. That could be characterized as a parody because it was funny. We all thought it was funny. She thought it was funny.

**—DAVID WEISMAN**

She was absolutely committed the same way David and I were committed. Come hell or high water, she was gonna do this, and this had to get done. It had to get finished, didn't matter what. That involved tremendous bravery on her part because of the fact that she was willing, when she was letting it all hang out, I don't like that expression, but when she was being forthright with the bare face of her, the raw part of her soul in this expression, that took a hell of a lot of guts to dissemble herself that way.

**—JOHN PALMER**

I know that she wanted to tell some kind of story, and I don't know if she was unable to put it into words, strictly into words, or if, maybe, it was once again like a total package. You have to see a little bit of her artwork, and a little bit of her film work, and a little bit of the things that she wrote down, as well as the things that she said, in order to put it all together. But the theme of communication—it's just, like, share who you are, and don't be afraid to let people know that you're human. That you've failed at some things, that you're maybe not as good at some things as you are at others, and to build people up to encourage them and to hopefully live to your potential. She wanted to reach the heights. She wanted that recognition, and she thought that she had something for everyone. But I know there was an element of ego in there. There always is an element of ego. We're just built that way.

**—MICHAEL POST**

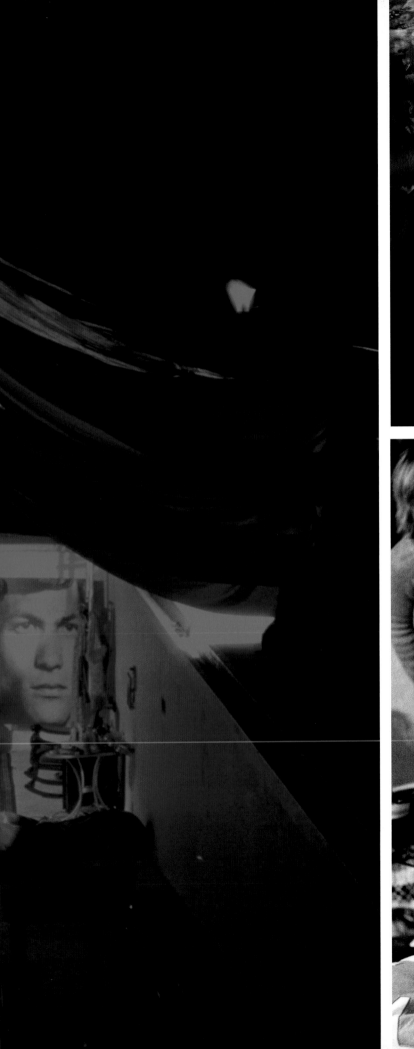

CIAO! MANHATTAN
COLOR SHOOT

Last lifeboat from the sixties from New York, that's what it was. Pulled up paddlin' in an old beater Mercedes, great big one, and they had scarves around their necks and they talked a hundred miles an hour. They were extremely focused and intense. That was very different, you know, Southern California, cool-jazz-beatnik phase became hippie phase, and it wasn't really cool to be too excited about shit.

**—JEFF BRIGGS**

I convinced John with these phone calls I would make, I would go to a bank and get a bag of quarters and keep feeding the long distance, you know, pay phone to London and spent hours on the phone with John to London and convinced him it was time to come over. I don't have a clue how I did that. It was, like, inconceivable, but I guess he had it in him that he wanted to, so there was the convergence, Kjell Rostad drove out in my big Mercedes with Eduardo Lopez de Romaña, and we all lived in this two-bedroom bungalow out in the valley on this crazy dragon-lady's estate, which later inpired shooting in the pool. John arrived with Janet, and we lived there and started to look for money.

**—DAVID WEISMAN**

The first time I ever met Edie I was just this little kid, you know, so I was all excited. I mean, I really didn't know what to say to her at the time, but she was very warming. She would talk to you and just look at you and "you're all that and who are you and I'm so glad to meet you and hi" and just charming and sparkling and all of these things. You know, I had never encountered anything like that, like, up close . . .

**—WESLEY HAYES**

Even in her most far-out sort of state she had tremendous appeal. That's what was so incredible about her, is that she could be really spaced beyond belief and she still could put a sentence together that would blow your brains out . . . That one-upmanship kind of thing.

**—MICHAEL POST**

In December 1970 we began filming the color footage in Santa Barbara. I asked Roger Vadim to play the doctor. He drove up with his pal Christian Marquand, the two of them flirting with Edie during the shoot, a whole routine. These two debonair French directors enthralled with Edie and she enthralled with them. But it took a turn where Edie really felt that Vadim and her had reached an understanding—he'd just broken up with Jane Fonda, and Edie somehow saw herself as his next muse. Brigitte Bardot, Catherine Deneuve, other great European beauties of the mid-twentieth century—Vadim was the Casanova of his era. He clearly saw something in Edie. So there was a day trip out to see him in Malibu. I remember him asking, "Da-veed, do you think Edith likes cracked crab?" Vadim always believed Edie just needed a little bit of love. All through the color shoot Edie kept asking, "When is Vadim coming?" The night she went home with him, I got the phone call at 3 A.M. from Vadim. "Can you come and collect Edith? It's a bit much." I sent Michael Post.

**—DAVID WEISMAN**

The pool shoot—this was an extremely difficult, challenging period of time. The people that had this enormous focus from the outset, John Palmer, David Weisman, Kjell Rostad, Eduardo Romaña. Their depth of focus served them well when they got to that point. Because things began to spin.

**—JEFF BRIGGS**

They liked her, but then they got scared. There was too much of her that was disturbed for people.

**—JANET PALMER**

It was a slow-motion emergency. Something about David Weisman and John Palmer that they knew and realized, and so that's why the film was going through the camera. It was hard to stop at any one instant and say, "Why is the film going through the camera right now? What are we all doing right now, at this instant?" It was hard to do that, but somehow they conceived. And Edie, too. Edie more than anything. Edie so intensely, because she was all in. You'd look around in the lifeboat and you could pick out, "Yeah, you know this girl probably ain't gonna make it." You

could kinda pick her out. It was sad as hell. It was sad as hell.

**—JEFF BRIGGS**

There's some aspect of where she understands some profound sense of damage that's foundational. And she goes on despite this. And that's deeply part of the little secret in a human. She knows how to find that in others, and it's an unspoken communication that she can go to, which is one of her secret little magic tricks.

**—JOHN PALMER**

I used to fight with her about her pills, because I used to always find that she hadn't taken them, which I think killed her in the end . . . She used to save them up . . . And then if she liked me that day, she'd say, "I'm going to take a lot of pills today," and I would go in, like, four times in the night and check that she hadn't died or something.

**—JANET PALMER**

Because we were always afraid, of course, that she would slit her wrists. We'd been warned by her shrink and the previous nurse. No razor blades . . . That she would attempt suicide.

**—JOHN PALMER**

Edie could only sort of play herself or play herself in her memories, and so it was a reentering process, the mind keeps on going back. It's a form of mental illness and Edie, at that point, sort of had a lot of that in her personality. There were always flashbacks to another era. It's really what became the pool sequences. I mean, they were not really invented. Edie already had that in her. It was like an inability to form new experiences and new connections and new relationships. It was always sort of like couching the past and going back.

—EDUARDO LOPEZ DE ROMAÑA

I mean, there had been some real meanness there, and she kept on going back to that, and she couldn't forgive her father. She couldn't forgive, you know, the death of her brother, and so it was all this luggage from way back and . . . it came back in every conversation . . . I think that a key ingredient in functional behavior is to have a firewall and say this is bad, I'm gonna put this aside, and I'm gonna forget it.

—EDUARDO LOPEZ DE ROMAÑA

The death of her father, the fact that she wasn't able to be there when her father passed away caused her some very . . . I remember her saying that was a source of her discontent.

—MICHAEL POST

Her shrink felt that it was critical that she see none of the family. Ever. For some reason he felt that it was important that she not see her mother, ever. Janet had a good relationship with her mother. She'd speak to her on the phone. And I think the mother, in the final analysis, really quite cared about her. But she was just kind of incapable, . . . in dealing with Edie. She used to write her lovely notes, and Edie'd pretty much flip out . . . She'd sort of create a self-induced state of flip out. Just "I love you and I care about you and I hope you're well" . . . I think the mother really quite cared.

—JOHN PALMER

Next thing I knew, she came out of the bathroom, and she was displaying her wrists to us.

She locked herself up in the bathroom. Yeah, I can remember that . . . She might have made some noise about it. It's very hard for me to remember because it all happened so fast. Yeah, she was really proud of it.

—JOHN PALMER

And this is what growth is all about. Why do people stop developing, or, like they stop the way you can rate their, psychologically, their development? Where they stop, and just from being children to maybe stopping at a very adolescent age, and they stay there until they die. Physically die. I mean, they react adolescently. They don't change. They don't develop. They don't—it's that continual read, that process which is the total threat for the ego.

—EDIE

**GHOSTS**

It was more of a "Oh, I'm uptight about going to this or that event, so let me take the 'edge' off of my anxiety" . . . In other words, "Let me have a drink or a bottle of wine or let me have, like, a half or a third of my nightly medications, you know, so that I can look like I'm totally cool about all this . . . like it does not faze me in the least." You know, to me, now that's part of living, you know, there are things to get excited about and then there are things that, you know, you need to

remain calm for. But it seems like that's an emergency now, not take the edge off. You know, that was kind of it. "Let's get as jacked up as we possibly can in order to project the image of maintaining as even a keel as we possibly can." In other words, "I want to get really balled up and wired and everything, but I want to pretend, make everybody else think that it doesn't even faze me." Some like power over the power, you know?

—MICHAEL POST

It was like she could see, just out of her reach, she could see how it could have been her, what she could offer, the fine quality of thought that she was capable of.

—JEFF BRIGGS

I don't think Edie had ever given up on a regular, on at least the concept of having a regular, easygoing kind of a life. Although it might have been a little out of her reach, she would emulate that.

—JEFF BRIGGS

But, I mean, I haven't been in love with anyone in years and years. But I have a certain amount of faith that it'll come.

—EDIE

You can smell everybody's blossoms in the air if you walk down their street with the oak trees over ya, and we'd hold hands and swing our hands, and she's wearing a little flower-print dress, a little bit gauzy, and maybe she knew the butcher by name, and he's got on a white apron . . . I remember step by step. I remember the cracks in the sidewalk and steppin' over 'em, because she was so intense. She was extremely intense with the projection of her emotion . . . She'd cook a nice little dinner, pork and potatoes and some parsley sprinkled on there. Fry me pork chops in a frying pan. Find me anybody else, Edie Sedgwick fried 'em pork chops in a frying pan. It was like a demonstration: "This is what it could have been for a person like me" . . . Playin' house. Sad as hell. A very honest pantomime.

—JEFF BRIGGS

Part of her existence is . . . a deeply poignant and sad, very mature understanding of her own permanent unrequitedness, that she's yearning for in a deeply profound and sincere way.

—JOHN PALMER

She would allude to the fact that love was something that would be pleasant, that she'd be looking forward to the idea.

—JOHN PALMER

On the day that John and I got married in Santa Barbara, Edie needed a lot of attention . . . and I hate to use American words like "demanding," but she was quite pushy. She wanted the attention. She wanted this for breakfast. She wanted that. And you sort of understood why, so it wasn't so hard to bear. And then we went to the church . . . We did her all up, and we got her all ready and then we got, I remember we dressed all the dogs up, and we got down there. She said, "Oh, am I getting married?" And I said, "No, you're not, I am."

—JANET PALMER

When John Palmer and Janet Brooke were married, Edie Sedgwick stood right behind Janet Palmer. Janet took her vows, and Edie mouthed all the words. And that would break your heart right then and there. Because you could see that she was reaching out and making her little echo of something that probably wasn't gonna work for her.

—JEFF BRIGGS

Did I ever feel she was going to throw herself off a bridge? No. Did I feel that she could conceivably injure herself fatally? Yes. Did I think the risk of that was extremely high? Not terribly. Because she didn't exhibit the resolve. She'd never willfully cast herself in front of a bus or fall in front of a subway train. But because she was killing herself in front of your very eyes by virtue of her disorders, yes.

—JOHN PALMER

She was there [Cottage Hospital] and being medicated and, of course, they were classic cuckoo's nest: Walk around, it's pill time, and here the nurse or the orderly dispenses out this hour's ration of medication and then, of course, the drugs that would walk in off of the street. I'm certain that that's where a lot of the extra drugs came from, and she was, she was doing the self-medication thing. I'd been "scared straight" so to speak, and I didn't really want it, and I didn't understand why she was there, and yet at the same time kind of defeating the purpose of her being there, by her behavior. So, yeah, I would question her about it, and she just kind of, she'd say things like, "Let's go to this club and we'll dance and we can go out." So it was like, "I need to dance something out." The catharsis.

I need to dance something out as a catharsis. I need to write something out as a catharsis for my own well-being, my own mental health. I need to talk to my therapist as a catharsis to purge myself of whatever it is that's bothering me or driving me to this kind of behavior. So there were a number of things that she would say and also do, and it was usually under the guise of "I need" to do this, not "Hey, let's just go have a good time." It's "Michael, I need to do this. I need to get this out of my system." After a while I thought, "I need? I need?" I mean, nobody needs what you're telling me you need. You've gotta be sick to think that I'm actually going to believe this, that you need to go to Isla Vista and you need to shoot some heroin. No, I'm not buying that. I don't believe you need that.

—MICHAEL POST

Here's the thing, and it was clear as a bell: It didn't have to be that way. Fate is not written in stone the day you're born. But somehow she was on that path, and she wasn't getting off. But if you really watched her, sometimes she'd look over and it was almost like she was giving you a wink or a glint, like a little high side, you know. The significance . . . that she realized the spot she was in, and that she was playing that role.

—JEFF BRIGGS

She said, "I don't know why I go. We never seem to get anywhere. He never tells me what's wrong with me." I do think she thought there was something wrong with her.

—JANET PALMER

Yeah, and then with those eyes and, my god, if I don't, if I don't take her to Isla Vista, then is she just going to dispose of me? It's like, use once or abuse once. No longer necessary? Throw away. I didn't want to be thrown away. I didn't want to lose her because I became consumed by her.

—MICHAEL POST

I thought Michael Post was very sweet . . . I thought he was a very kind boy. I think we were all quite pleased that she had found somebody who didn't run away from her.

—JANET PALMER

MARRIAGE

Before we were married, for two years, or almost two years, nightly, nightly I had just passionate and almost prophetic dreams about Edie and myself, and sensory dreams. Having her sit in my lap and feeling—remembering in the dream that I could feel heat or softness, or smell a fragrance or an aroma, or feel the chill of this . . . The sensory, the sensations I went through in my dream life about her, I was just consumed, and I thought, "I am going to marry this woman. There's no doubt about it. She's going to be the first woman that I ever have sex with, that I ever consummate sex with" . . . Sure enough, she was the first woman, sure enough, I did marry her, so in one sense, yeah, my dreams. She was the woman of my dreams.

—MICHAEL POST

I was there [at the wedding] and she was, perhaps, the happiest I've ever seen her in her life. She was all in white, and there was a certain radiance that, perhaps, still shone through in spite of it all. And I've never seen her smile more than at that wedding. I mean, it was something very special for her. She was all in white, and it was a simple, beautiful ceremony.

—EDUARDO LOPEZ DE ROMAÑA

I actually think I was in love with what I believed to be her potential. The person that I could see that she had the possibility to be.

—MICHAEL POST

She used to finish off quite a lot of sentences, "Well, I'll just kill myself."

—JANET PALMER

I knew that she was the one. There were things that I could give her, at least I hoped and thought and felt there were, and things that I wanted from her, and I thought she could give to me. In other words, we could share. But given the kind of, the age difference, the experiential difference, and the, I guess, socioeconomic differences in our backgrounds, it was, perhaps, a little bit too much to ask for. There were a number of rocky times in that short, not even four months we were married, that were extremely challenging. I remember one time I, it was about pills, or alcohol, or something—or "Let's go here." I didn't want to go there. I didn't want to drag myself through another sleepless night, or go to the hospital, slashing wrists . . . I did that a couple of times when Edie slashed her wrists. I had to go to the emergency hospital, get her sewn up, do those kinds of things, and I was kind of, like, weary of it. That was, like, less than four months into our marriage.

—MICHAEL POST

I think she was always leaving him, even when she got married to him, wasn't she? I mean, I think she thought marriage would give her some sort of independence from parents. I think that, like a lot of people, she thought it would change her life somehow. If she thought that far ahead, but I don't think she did. She really liked getting married, though . . . When she got married, it was so beautiful.

—JANET PALMER

There were times that I was totally convinced that Edie was in love with me . . . I think she wanted me to kind of be a nursemaid, a lover, a boyfriend, a father, a brother, a husband. You know, all of those things, but I was incapable of it, because I wasn't her brother, and I wasn't her father, and I wasn't her psychiatrist, and I wasn't a number of those things. But yet she wanted me to be, and I just couldn't fill all those roles for her. That led to problems, and then the frustration, and then, of course, the quick escape: "Let's get loaded, forget about it."

—MICHAEL POST

We talked about having kids, and, as a matter of fact, she thought she might even be pregnant there at the very end. And it was kind of like, well, we've kind of tried a number of things . . . maybe a child would bring us closer together. And you know, "I'm into my late 20s now, Michael, and maybe it's time for me to have kids if I can at this point."

—MICHAEL POST

I remember driving one time, driving back to Santa Barbara from this ranch, and she says, "I want to drive." And I was going, "Oh, god, I want to live. I want us to live." You know? And I went, "Okay." The little highways, you've got a whole lot of curves, and sometimes you can get a little bit off the road and not crash into the mountain, but just go up it a little bit. The first couple of times we just went up

on the shoulder, the little curb thing. I went, Okay, I'm not gonna say anything. I'm not gonna jump out, and go, "I'm scared, all right, slow down." I just thought, maybe, there's a couple of curves here, maybe we need to be cautious about how we drive through them, and then got way high up off the road, leaning to the right because the car will tip over if we lean the other direction. So it was like I had my daughter in the car, and I was letting her drive for the first time. I didn't want to be severe, and I didn't want to dash her hopes and aspirations, so I just gave her some rein, you know, kind of those little fatherly things, and maybe she wanted or needed more rein.

—MICHAEL POST

That last night I can't remember exactly if she said, "We're not going to be together much longer." Or "I don't think we're gonna be together much longer." Or maybe even "I don't want to be," you know, "I think we're going in different directions." Or "We're not both going in the same direction." Words to that effect. That hurt me, and I thought, okay, I guess to save a little face or something, you know how your ego will kind of kick in? It's like, okay, yeah, sure. I get you well. I bring you back to fame and fortune, and this is my—this is the gratitude I get for it.

—MICHAEL POST

He said, "Oh, I'm fine, but Edie's not moving." And I said, "Well, have you held a mirror up?" And he said, "Yes, I've done all that." And I said, "Well, have you called the police?" And he said, "I don't know how to." And I think John called the police from New York to Santa Barbara, and we kept him on the phone, and he was crying and saying, "Nobody will ever know how much I loved her."

—JANET PALMER

David listened and listened and listened, and then he put the phone down with his hand over the mouthpiece and said, "Edie's dead." Everyone stood there. It was a sense of shock . . . David spoke to Michael for a few minutes, and then I spoke to Michael for a few minutes. I read recently in an interview I gave from decades ago that I remember him saying, "I killed her, I killed my baby." I can't be sure, something like that, but he was saying it over and over. Then we asked him about the whole situation, on the phone. Michael said they'd been to that Santa Barbara museum thing the night before . . . and a party afterwards or something, I don't know. He said that she'd been taking something, or she'd had too much of something, or something like that and she just never woke up. He was lying next to her, and he was crying, terribly, and he tried to wake her up, but she wouldn't wake up. And I believe the first thing he did was, he called us. The only thing I remember now is the feeling, and the cold light streaming in the morning window . . . the feeling of all of us—in her death.

—JOHN PALMER

It was such a sad thing. I remember I'd set my alarm for, like, seven o'clock or something cause I had a French class that I think started at eight o'clock. But I knew that, having gotten home at, like, two A.M., whatever, after some drinks and the emotional draining and exhaustion of the conversation . . . at this cocktail party, and also with Edie, I knew I wasn't getting up for this French class or test, whatever it was. I woke up, turned the alarm clock off, went back to sleep, never even looked around, and then woke up later and noticed that Edie was, as I kind of was getting up I kind of noticed . . . Is she in the same position as she was when she went to sleep? Usually she was up earlier than I was. I turned over and moved, and it was like the rigor mortis was already playing its card and taking effect, and she was partially stiff, and I bolted up. All of a sudden I just bug out. I'm going, "Oh my god. She's died. She's dead on—on me, you know." And I started thinking—mouth-to-mouth resuscitation, what do you do? I said, "I believe in miracles," and "God, let me give her the breath of life and bring her back to life." Held her nose, breathed into her mouth, tried to breathe into her mouth. It was like getting lockjaw, and instantly in my nostrils the smell of death.

—MICHAEL POST

When I knew her, she was not of this Earth. She was, indeed, never of this Earth. She was born of madness and suffering and declined into madness and suffering. But she had a period when the sun shone for her, when life was smiling. And she was smiling with it.

—DONALD LYONS

## REACTIONS TO HER DEATH

I didn't think this was going to happen to her, what happened to her. I thought she was a major soul.

—L. M. KIT CARSON

I think there's one thing that can be said about Edie, though. I think she exemplifies in many ways the sixties, which is really the most puzzling era.

—GEORGE PLIMPTON

Was New York too much for Edie? Possibly. I think the times were too much for her. Could've happened in San Francisco, could've happened in L.A., could've happened in New York. I mean, that's what the times were all about. They were about going crazy. Legitimately, everybody was going crazy and, of course, the climate made it possible. Drugs made it possible.

—JUDY FEIFFER

You know what? There were times when there was almost a month of sobriety and just getting everything together. God, things were nice, you know. We'd come up here [the ranch]. We spent a lot of time up here during those times, and she wasn't hitting mother's medicine cabinet, and it was great just to be healthy and have the horizons expand. Being up here is great and, you know, starry nights and, you know, sunny days and riding horses or just walking around looking at all the wildlife and just natural beauty. It was fabulous.

—MICHAEL POST

She had a lot to say. She had an enormous quality. It was almost like some of the things she went through, it was as if to say, "This is what can come of the best of us. This is what can happen to the best of us."

—JEFF BRIGGS

I was not surprised that she had passed away. I was surprised at how she passed away. She finally found love, and was with her new husband, and they went to bed one evening, and when he woke up the next morning, she didn't wake up. That was how Edie passed away. I do remember going to the funeral. Me and Jeff went to the funeral together, and I remember driving up to Santa Barbara and standing in the back, behind the crowd of people.

—BOB MARGOULEFF

It was so cold. It was sunny. Maybe only a row and a half, the first row and a half of pews had people in it . . . It was a long time before I even remembered that Robert Margouleff was with me because it was like one of these tunnel-vision things. I'm so sorry, you know. It seems so stupid. Of course she had a support network or something, up to some level, and professionals and medical people and whatnot, but I don't care. It still seems like such a tragic waste, you know.

—JEFF BRIGGS

It was sad but not shocking. There was something about Edie that said, "This is a one-act play. It's not going to go on forever."

—FRED EBERSTADT

I think she's one of those people that you think back on and what flashes in your mind is an instant image. You remember friends who've gone or died. You remember certain aspects of them. You remember *the* image of Edie, the face. Large eyes. Painless, the pale hair. And then you remember the sadness, too, this exquisite young girl who had been so troubled, had so much help, and was extinguished by what she couldn't control.

—GEORGE PLIMPTON

Why Edie? I mean, look at her, she was so beautiful. She represented the wildness and the abandon and, in a sense, what turned out to be the suicides of the sixties.

—JANE HOLZER

# EVErythinG

that happened to me has been a
paradox for life. The very things that
I should have done would have been
the trap. The very things I might have
given in to, that demanded, that said,
this is your life. I mean, this is your
only way to survive, are the things
I fought hardest to end. 'Cause I
believed in something else. You have
to work like mad to make people
understand . . . Even if I don't make
it, you know, I really insist on believ-
ing, and then I fall off the edge
because there's nobody else to follow
it. And I would just fall off the edge . . .

—EDIE

She later went on to be the doorperson at Max's Kansas City.

**SEPP DONAHOWER** is a rock-and-roll promoter and entrepreneur who, as a college student in 1967, drove cross-country with Edie to California.

**BOB DYLAN**, a legendary singer/songwriter, met Edie soon after she moved to New York in 1964.

**BURT GLINN** worked as a photographer for *Life*, and as a freelancer, became an associate member of Magnum, later serving as the group's president.

**TOMMY GOODWIN** was Edie's friend in Cambridge and briefly her chauffeur in New York. He worked on the crew of both *Ciao! Manhattan* and PBS's *American Family* series in Santa Barbara, where he encountered Edie at a party the night she died.

**BETSEY JOHNSON**, an international fashion designer, was the chief designer for Paraphernalia in 1965, where Edie was her first fitting model. She also designed some costumes for the black-and-white sequences of *Ciao! Manhattan*. She was once married to John Cale.

**LARISSA** was a regular at Ondine's, Max's Kansas City, and the Factory. In the sixties, she lived at the Chelsea hotel. She currently designs fur coats.

## TIMELINE

**APRIL 20, 1943:** Edie is born.

**FALL 1956:** Edie goes to boarding school, the Katherine Branson School, near San Francisco.

**SPRING 1957:** Edie returns from boarding school and stays on ranch.

**FALL 1958:** Edie attends St. Timothy's school in Stevenson, Maryland.

**SPRING 1959:** Edie returns from St. Timothy's.

**FALL 1962?:** Edie goes to Silver Hill, followed by Bloomingdale.

**SPRING 1963:** Edie gets a day pass to leave Bloomingdale, gets pregnant, and eventually has an abortion.

**FALL 1963:** Edie goes to Cambridge.

**MARCH 4, 1964:** Minty Sedgwick dies.

**APRIL 20, 1964:** Edie's 21st birthday party is held at the Harvard Boat House. She gets her maternal grandmother's trust fund.

**SUMMER 1964:** Edie drives to New York with Gordon Baldwin and moves into her grandmother's apartment.

**LATE FALL 1964:** Edie moves from her grandmother's place into an apartment in the East 60s, between 5th and Madison Avenues.

**DECEMBER 1964:** Edie meets Bob Dylan and Bob Neuwirth.

**CHRISTMAS 1964:** Edie returns to the ranch for the holidays.

**DECEMBER 31, 1964:** Bobby Sedgwick crashes his motorcycle into a bus; Edie is in a car crash in California.

**JANUARY 12, 1965:** Bobby Sedgwick dies of his injuries.

**MARCH 26, 1965:** Edie meets Andy Warhol in Lester Persky's apartment at a birthday party for Tennessee Williams.

**MARCH 1965:** *Bitch* is filmed; *Vinyl* is filmed.

**APRIL 1965:** *Horse* is filmed.

**APRIL 9, 1965:** Edie and Andy attend a preview at the Museum of Modern Art.

**APRIL 1965:** *Face* is filmed. *Poor Little Rich Girl* is filmed.

**APRIL 25, 1965:** 50 Most Beautiful People Party is thrown by Lester Persky at the Factory.

**APRIL 30-EARLY MAY 1965:** Edie, Andy, Chuck, and Gerard go to Paris, London, Madrid, and Tangier. Andy opens a show at the Sonnabend Gallery in Paris, announces that he intends to quit painting to focus on underground filmmaking.

**MAY 3-8, 1965:** Dylan and Neuwirth travel to London, film the documentary *Dont Look Back*.

**MAY-JULY 1965:** *Restaurant* and *Beauty No. 2* are filmed.

**JUNE 1965:** *Kitchen* is filmed.

**JUNE 1965:** *Afternoon* is filmed.

**JUNE 15-16, 1965:** Dylan records "Like a Rolling Stone."

**JUNE 19-20, 1965:** *Poor Little Rich Girl* and *Vinyl* premiere at Astor Place Playhouse (Cinemateque) on a double bill.

**JUNE-JULY 1965:** *Space* is filmed.

JULY 1965: *Factory Diaries* is filmed.

JULY 1965: *Prison* is filmed.

JULY 17, 1965: *Beauty No. 2* premieres at Astor Place (Cinemateque).

JULY 26, 1965: *New York Times* publishes an article headlined "Edie Pops Up as Newest Star."

AUGUST 1965: *Outer and Inner Space* is filmed.

AUGUST 1965: *Vogue* article pegs Edie as a "Youthquaker."

NOVEMBER 1965: Bob Dylan marries Sara Lownds.

NOVEMBER 26, 1965: *Life* publishes an article about Edie titled "Girl with the Black Tights."

DECEMBER 6, 1965: Max's Kansas City opens.

DECEMBER 1965: *Lupe* is filmed.

LATE DECEMBER 1965: Edie and John Cale begin a relationship that lasts about a month.

JANUARY 13, 1966: Edie performs with the Velvet Underground at Delmonico's for the New York Society for Clinical Psychiatry.

JANUARY 25, 1966: Dylan begins recording "Leopard-Skin Pill-Box Hat."

FEBRUARY 13, 1966: the *New York Times* publishes photograph of Edie, Chuck, Andy in street.

FEBRUARY 1966: Edie and Andy argue at the Gingerman.

FEBRUARY 1966: Edie "leaves" Andy.

MARCH 3, 1966: *Kitchen* premieres at Cinemateque.

MARCH 8, 1966: Dylan begins recording "Just Like a Woman."

APRIL 10, 1966: Edie makes first non-Warhol film with Bob Neuwirth.

JULY 1966: Dylan crashes his motorcycle.

OCTOBER 17, 1966: Edie's apartment on 63rd Street burns.

NOVEMBER 1966: Edie allegedly films a Warhol movie starring Rene Ricard called *The Andy Warhol Story*.

LATE 1966: Edie moves to the Chelsea hotel.

CHRISTMAS 1966: Edie goes to California for the holidays; her parents have her committed to a hospital psychiatric ward.

EARLY 1967: Edie returns to New York and the Chelsea.

EARLY 1967: Bob Neuwirth leaves Edie.

MARCH 26, 1967: Central Park be-in; *Ciao! Manhattan* shoot begins.

APRIL 1967: Edie's Chelsea hotel room burns.

LATE SPRING-EARLY SUMMER 1967: Edie films *Ondine and Edie* with Andy.

JUNE 1967: Edie drives with friends to California.

SUMMER 1967: Edie moves to "the Castle" with Nico, Jim Morrison, others.

AUGUST 1967: Edie makes *Lulu*.

OCTOBER 23, 1967: Francis "Fuzzy" Sedgwick dies.

OCTOBER 1967: Edie begins a series of hospitalizations in New York and lives intermittently at the Warwick hotel.

LATE FALL 1968: Edie's mother removes her from the hospital and brings her home to stay on the ranch; she eventually moves into an apartment in Isla Vista.

SUMMER 1969: Edie goes to Cottage Hospital psychiatric ward after getting busted for spilling pills in front of a cop and then kicking him; she meets Michael Post.

DECEMBER 1970-JANUARY 1971: Second part of *Ciao! Manhattan* shot in Santa Barbara and Los Angeles.

JANUARY-JUNE 1971: Edie undergoes shock therapy.

JULY 24, 1971: Edie and Michael Post wed.

NOVEMBER 15, 1971: Edie attends the filming of *An American Family*.

NOVEMBER 16, 1971: Edie dies.

Library of Congress Cataloging-in-Publication
Data:

Painter, Melissa.
Edie : girl on fire / By Melissa Painter and
David Weisman.
p. cm.
Includes bibliographical references.
ISBN 0-8118-5526-0
1. Photography of women. 2. Sedgwick,
Edie—Portraits. I. Weisman, David. II. Title.
TR681.W6P35 2006
791.4302'8092—dc22
[B] 2006015145

ISBN-10: 0-8118-5526-0
ISBN-13: 978-0-8118-5526-6

Manufactured in Hong Kong.

CD original recording by John Palmer.★
CD edited by Mark Plunkett.★
CD soundmix by Jonathan Orozco.★

Designed by Ayako Akazawa.★

Distributed in Canada by Raincoast Books★
9050 Shaughnessy Street
Vancouver, British Columbia V6P 6E5

10 9 8 7 6 5 4 3 2 1

Chronicle Books LLC★
680 Second Street
San Francisco, California 94107
www.chroniclebooks.com

Front cover photo by Terry Stevenson, ©
Agita Productions Inc.★
Back cover photo by Burt Glinn, © Burt Glinn/
Magnum Photos.★

Quotations by Bob Neuwirth, Lily Saarinen,
Jonathan Sedgwick, and John Anthony Walker
from the book Edie: American Girl, edited by
Jean Stein with George Plimpton, copyright
© 1982 by Jean Stein and Hadada, Inc.★
Quotations by Andy Warhol from the books
The Philosophy of Andy Warhol (From A to B
and Back Again) by Andy Warhol, copyright ©
1975 by Andy Warhol; and POPism: The Warhol
Sixties by Andy Warhol and Pat Hackett, copy-
right © 1980 by Andy Warhol.★
Quotations by Henry Geldzahler, Ondine,
and Patti Smith (p. 106) from the book
Factory Made: Warhol and the Sixties by
Steven Watson, copyright © 2003 by Steven
Watson.★
Quotation by Bob Dylan from "Bob Dylan: Not
Like a Rolling Stone," interview by Scott
Cohen, originally published in Spin magazine,
1985, reprinted in the book Younger Than
That Now: The Collected Interviews of Bob
Dylan by James Whitfield Ellison, compilation
copyright © 2004 by Thunder's Mouth
Press.★
"Everyone knew she was the real heroine of
Blonde on Blonde" from "Edie Sedgwick (1943–
1971)" by Patti Smith, from the book Seventh
Heaven by Patti Smith, copyright © 1972 by
Telegraph Books.★

## Photo Credits ★

BOB ADELMAN, pp. 52, 55 (top), 57, 60 (top), 62, 63, 70 (bottom), 71, 83, 95, 99, 101 (top), 112★ COLLECTION OF THE ANDY WARHOL MUSEUM, pp. 22 (bottom), 58, 72 (bottom)★ HAL BOUCHER, p. 182★ JEFF BRIGGS, p. 164 (left)★ RICHARD DAVIS, pp. 165 (bottom right), 169 (bottom), 173, 174, 175 (bottom)★ CALEB DESCHANEL, p. 161 (top)★ FRED EBERSTADT, pp. 4, 34, 35, 74, 75, 96, 97, 109, 113, 117, 118, 119, 120, 121, 122, 191★ NAT FARBMAN, p. 25★ DANNY FIELDS COLLECTION, pp. 16, 20 (right), 21 (left), 28★ NAT FINKELSTEIN, pp. 43 (top), 45 (top), 46, 47, 48, 49, 50, 85 (top), 90 (left), 124, 125, 127 (top), 128, 155★ JIM GALETE, pp. 141 (left), 146 (bottom), 148 (left), 151, 152★ BURT GLINN, pp. 77, 78, 79, 80, back cover★ SAM GREEN, p. 107 (left)★ JIM HUGHES (photos), NEW YORK DAILY NEWS, p. 153★ LISA LAW, p. 160★ DONALD MACSORLEY, pp. 137, 138★ DAVID C. MARKS, p. 10★ RICHARD MARX, p. 87★ STAN MAYS, p. 68★ DAVID MCCABE, p. 88★ PAUL MORRISSEY, p. 98 (top left)★ BILLY NAME, pp. 29, 42, 43 (bottom), 44, 56, 59, 61, 65, 82, 102, 105 (top right), 106, 127 (bottom), 135 (left)★ JOHN PALMER, pp. 6, 10, 81, 86, 89, 90 (right), 94, 101 (middle, bottom), 103, 105 (top left), 134, 135 (right), 136, 139, 140, 141 (top right), 143, 146 (top), 147 (right), 148 (right), 149, 156, 157, 161 (bottom) 177, 178, 179, 181 (bottom left), 183★ GIANNI PENATI, pp. 107 (right column), 108★ EDUARDO LOPEZ DE ROMAÑA, pp. 11, 164 (top right), 180★ STEVE SCHAPIRO, pp. 13, 72 (top)★ JERRY SCHATZ-BERG, pp. 1, 129, 130, 131, 132, 133★ LARRY SCHOCK, pp. 166, 167, 172, 175 (top)★ JONA-THAN SEDGWICK, pp. 18, 19★ ENZO SELERIO, p. 45 (bottom)★ STEPHEN SHORE, pp. 27 (bottom), 39 (top), 40, 41, 51, 53, 54, 55 (bottom), 60 (bottom), 64, 66, 67, 69, 70 (top), 73, 84, 85 (bottom), 92, 98 (top right, bottom), 100, 104, 105 (bottom), 110, 111, 126★ TERRY STEVENSON, front cover, pp. 91, 114, 141 (bottom right), 142, 144, 145, 147 (left), 149, 150, 186, 192★ SANDEE TALLEY-HANLINE COL-LECTION, p. 165 (bottom left)★ ANDY WARHOL, p. 58★ DAVID WEED, pp. 3, 162, 163, 164 (bottom right), 165 (top), 168, 169 (top), 170, 171★ DAVID WEISMAN COLLECTION, pp. 2, 17, 19 (right), 20 (left and center), 21 (right), 22 (top row), 23, 24, 25, 26, 27 (top), 30, 31, 32, 33, 39 (middle and bottom), 181 (top row, bottom right)★

## Photo Captions ★

P. 2: With Andy Warhol and Norelco video camera during filming of Inner and Outer Space, August 1965★ P. 3: With Wesley Hayes during Ciao! Manhattan color shoot, January, 1971★ P. 10: David Weisman★ P. 11: With Wesley Hayes★ P. 16: At Cambridge, 1963★ P. 17: At Silver Hill, 1962★ P. 18: At Cambridge, 1963 (photograph taken by brother Jonathan)★ P. 19: At Silver Hill★ P. 20: (left and center) Photobooth strip with Bartle Bull; (right) With Ed Hennessey★ P. 21: (right) With Bartle Bull★ P. 22: (top row) Edie's early artwork; (bottom) Sculpting in Cambridge★ P. 23: The Sedgwick family. Top row: Pamela, Bobby, Saucie. Bottom Row: Jonathan, Alice, Edie (on mother's lap), Kate, Francis, Suky (on father's lap), Minty★ P. 24: (top left) Edie on pony; (top right) Francis Sedgwick; (bottom) Francis Sedgwick's horse sculpture★ P. 25: Francis reading to the children (photograph appeared in Life magazine)★ P. 26: With Ed Hennessey★ P. 27: (top) Gordon Baldwin's apartment; (bottom) Ed Hennessey★ P. 30: Partying in Cambridge★ P. 31: At Silver Hill★ PP. 32-33: Edie's 21st birthday party at the Harvard Boat House★ PP. 34-35: Life magazine photo shoot in the Hamptons★ PP. 38-39: Drawing at the Factory★ P. 39: (middle and bottom) Early artwork★ P. 40: With Chuck Wein at the Factory★ P. 41: With Donald Lyons at The Scene★ PP. 42-43 (bottom): With (left to right) Eric Anderson, Donald Lyons, and Ed Hennessey during the filming of Space★ PP. 44-45: With (left to right) Gino Piserchio and Chuck Wein at the Factory★ P. 45: (bottom) Vogue magazine introduces Edie as "youth-quaker," August 1965★ PP. 46-50: During the filming of Lupe★ P. 51: (top and middle) The Factory; (bottom) Andy on the Factory couch★ P. 53: Billy Name cutting Edie's hair while Ondine tapes on the Factory fire escape★ P. 55: (bottom) With (foreground left to right) Ivy Nicholson, Chuck Wein★ P. 56: Filming Vinyl★ P. 57: With Chuck Wein and Andy in the Factory★ P. 58: Frames from one of Edie's screen tests★ P. 60: (bottom) With (left to right) Dorothy Dean, Donald Lyons, Chuck Wein, Andy Warhol, Bibbe Hansen, unknown, Stephen Shore, unknown, Pat Hartley, and unknown★ PP. 62-63: With Gino Piserchio and Andy during the filming of Beauty #2★ P. 66: With Andy and Chuck Wein at the Factory★

CREDITS

P. 68: With Andy at a press conference ★ P. 70: (bottom) With Andy and Bibbe Hansen at a restaurant ★ P. 71: With Andy at Al Roon's pool party "happening" ★ P. 72: (top) With Andy at a party ★ PP. 74-75: *Life* magazine photo shoot in the Hamptons ★ PP. 77-80: With Andy and Chuck Wein, for the *London Times* ★ P. 85: (top) With (left to right) Danny Williams, Andy, Lou Reed, Sterling Morrison, John Cale, Gerard Malanga, at Pana Grady's; (bottom) With Ondine at the Factory ★ P. 87: With Mick Jagger ★ PP. 90-91: During the *Ciao! Manhattan* b&w shoot, 1967 ★ P. 92: With Ondine during the filming of *Restaurant* ★ P. 94: The Cloisters wall in upper Manhattan, during *Ciao! Manhattan* b&w shoot ★ P. 95: With Gino Piserchio ★ PP. 96-97: Fred Eberstadt fashion shoot for *Life* magazine ★ P. 98: (top left) With Gerard Malanga ★ P. 99: (top) With Chuck Wein, Lester Persky in back ★ P. 101: (top) At a party with Fred Eberstadt and Andy ★ P. 104: Filming *Restaurant* ★ P. 105: (top left) With Gino Piserchio during *Ciao! Manhattan* b&w shoot ★ P. 107: (left) Andy's first retrospective at the Institute of Contemporary Art in Philadelphia; (right) For *Vogue*, March 1966 ★ P. 112: With Fred Eberstadt and Andy ★ P. 113: *Life* magazine fashion shoot in the Hamptons ★ P. 114: At Dr. Roberts' office, 1967, during *Ciao! Manhattan* b&w shoot ★ PP. 116-117: Hamptons disco ★ PP. 118-119: Fred Eberstadt fashion shoot for *Life* magazine ★ PP. 120-121: *Life* fashion shoot in the Hamptons ★ P. 124: Bob Dylan visits the Factory ★ P. 125: Bob Dylan filming his screen test ★ P. 127: (top) John Brockman, Andy Warhol, Bob Dylan ★ P. 128: With Andy and Gerard Malanga ★ PP. 129-133: Fashion shoot commissioned by Albert Grossman ★ P. 135: (left) Filming *Vinyl* ★ P. 136: Edie shopping at a Canal Street bazaar during *Ciao! Manhattan* b&w shoot, 1967 ★ P. 137: With Bobby Neuwirth during the *Lulu* shoot ★ P. 138: Edie as Lulu ★ P. 141: with Jane Holzer (left) and Gino Piserchio (bottom right) during the *Ciao! Manhattan* b&w shoot ★ P. 142: At Dr. Roberts' spa ★ P. 143: with judo instructor ★ P. 144: with Pat Hartley ★ P. 146: (bottom) With Allen Ginsberg ★ P. 147: (left) With Viva ★ P. 148: (left) With Paul America ★ P. 149: (top left) At Dr. Roberts' office with Charlie Baccis and Pat Hartley during *Ciao! Manhattan* b&w shoot; (top right) With Genevieve Charbin; (bottom) On a raft with Viva at Dr. Roberts' spa ★ P. 152: Edie with burnt hand from Chelsea hotel fire ★ P. 153: *New York Daily News* article about Edie's 63rd Street fire ★ P. 157: Edie during *Ciao! Manhattan* b&w shoot with wax figures ★ P. 160: Exterior of the Castle, Los Feliz, Los Angeles ★ P. 161: (top) Sepp Donahower (foreground) and friend with the Volkswagen Squareback that drove Edie west; (bottom) From *Ciao! Manhattan* b&w shoot in Fort Lee, New Jersey ★ P. 162: With Wesley Hayes on the set of *Ciao! Manhattan* color shoot ★ P. 164: (left) Janet and John Palmer on *Ciao! Manhattan* pool set; (top right) With David Weisman en route to San Francisco, September 1970 ★ PP. 164-165: (bottom) During *Ciao! Manhattan* color shoot in Fremont Place, Los Angeles ★ P. 165: (bottom left) Preacher Ewing at Hell's Angels biker funeral, Santa Barbara; (bottom right) Wesley Hayes ★ P. 168: *Ciao! Manhattan* pool set at Lucky Baldwin estate in Arcadia, California ★ P. 169: (bottom) With (left to right) John Palmer, Michael Post, and Kjell Rostad ★ P. 170: Wesley Hayes carrying Edie ★ P. 171: With (left to right) John Palmer and Kjell Rostad ★ P. 172: With Bob Margouleff ★ P. 174: (top) With (left to right) David Weisman, John Palmer, Wesley Hayes, and Kjell Rostad; (bottom left) John Palmer on set; (bottom right) Bob Margouleff and David Weisman ★ P. 175: (top left) David Weisman and John Palmer ★ P. 180: In Santa Barbara, 1969 ★ P. 181: (top row and bottom right) Edie's last apartment in Santa Barbara ★ PP. 182-183: Edie and Michael Post on their wedding day, July 24, 1971. ★

**ACKNOWLEDGMENTS**

Our producing partners on the feature film documentary *Edie: Girl on Fire* merit special citation: Michael Maiello (whose involvement with Edie's story and *Ciao! Manhattan* began as a sophomore at Arizona State University in 1973), Michael Lustig, Christopher Law, and Lu Bolognue Law. The project would have never happened without them. ★
Grateful acknowledgment to Robin Sedgwick for her keen insight; Harry Dwight Sedgwick for his candor; John Palmer, whose cinematic kinship with Edie and with beauty was the enigmatic secret behind the whole saga; Sarah Weiss, our intrepid research assistant, mystery-solver, and support system; and Jane Holzer for her constant friendship. Deep appreciation to Chuck Wein, Donald Lyons, and Danny Fields for connecting the dots; to Rene Ricard for his brilliant humor; Frederick Eberstadt, Burt Glinn, and Jerry Schatzberg, for supreme generosity and wisdom as well as beautiful photographs; to all other interviewees who generously shared their unique insights and memories: Gordon Baldwin, Jeff Briggs, Bartle Bull, L. M. Kit Carson, Eden Cale, Sepp Donahower, Judy Feiffer, Nat Finkelstein, Sam Green, Sally Grossman, Clinton Wesley Hayes, Ed Hennessey, Bibbe Hansen, Margot Head, Sybil Hebb, Susan Hoffman, Betsey Johnson, Heidi Julavitz, The Kills, Larissa, Richard Leacock, Avery Maher, Bob Margouleff, Chase Mellen III, Paul Morrissey, Justin Moyer, Billy Name, Victor Navasky, Ivy Nicholson, Janet Brooke Palmer, George Plimpton, Michael Post, Rossie Fisher Reed, Dominique Robertson, Eduardo Lopez de Romaña, Libby Titus, Ultra Violet, and Rufus Wainwright. To others close to Edie who kindly shared their insights off the record, we are indebted. ★
Gratitude also Matt Wrbican, Greg Burchard, Geralyn Huxley, and Greg Pierce at the Andy Warhol Museum; Stephen Shore, Jean Stein, and Steven Watson; Dominick Dunne, Robert Farren, Kjell Rostad, Fred Levinson, and the late Jean and Ruth Margouleff, for their contributions to *Ciao! Manhattan.* ★
Special credit and thanks to Katie Mohr for her insightful interview with Michael Post from 1999. ★
Thanks also to Callie Angell, Charles Atlas, Marshall Bell, Marcelo Bernardes, Raimondo Biffi, Milena Canonero, Kira Coplin, Kathi Doak, August Goulet, William Grey Harris, Gary Hustwit, Jessica Hundley, Ricardo Koraicho, Kevin Kushel, Timothy Stokes Merrill, Bill Mooney, Mauricio Padilha, Sam Pietsch, Gabriel Rotello, Leonard Schrader, Jackie Scissors, Joel Shapiro, Michael Shulman, Simon Smith, Laura Steele, Vincent van Haaf, the Weiss family, Dr. James Welles, and David Wills. ★
With special thanks to Paz de la Huerta, Carlos Davis, Judith Bruce, Frank Digiacomo, attorneys James O'Callahan and Graham Lipp-Smith of Girardi & Keese, Sam Weisman, Alan Selka, Graydon Carter and Robert Evans, for their roles in the project's quirky genesis. ★
With thanks for their love and support to Zachary Matz; Toby Posner and John, Lulu, and Zelda Adams; Jeremi Handrinos and Nadine, Micah, and Cyrus; Mark Plunkett and Butch III; Sandro and Alonzo Meallet; and Michael, Susan, and Josh Painter. ★
Special appreciation to the late Terry Stevenson, and to contributing photographers Bob Adelman, Jeff Briggs, Richard Davis, Frederick Eberstadt, Nat Finkelstein, Jim Galete, Burt Glinn, Lisa Law, Stan Mays, David McCabe, Paul Morrissey, Billy Name, Gianni Penati, Steve Schapiro, Jerry Schatzberg, Larry Schock, Enzo Sellerio, Stephen Shore, and David Weed, among others. This project honors the memories of Roger Vadim, Isabel Jewell, Coco Brown, Gino Piserchio, Manuel Puig, and Andy Warhol. ★
Finally, to Steve Mockus, Matt Robinson, Ayako Akazawa, Tera Killip, and Sarah Malarkey of Chronicle Books, for their faith and vision. ★

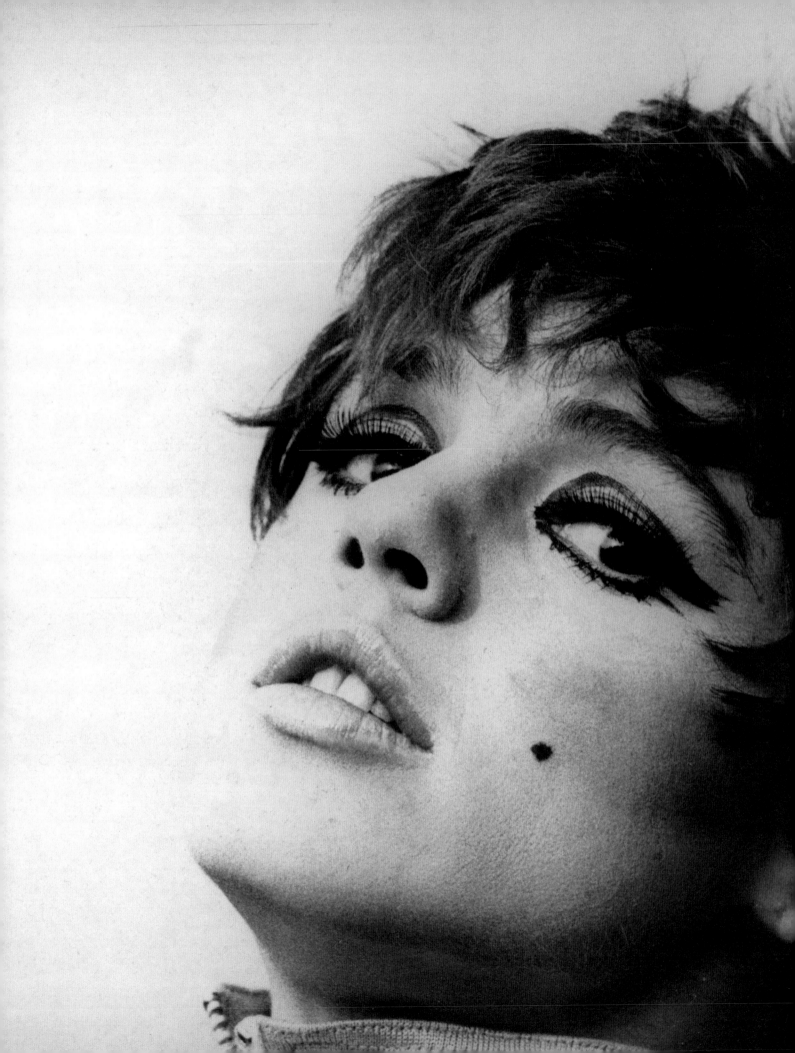